How to Start a
Movement
in Your Company

David Choe

Table of Contents

Preface

Changing from the bottom-up

In business literature the CEO-led transformation is a well-known plot line. General Electric is often cited as an example. In this case, CEO Jack Welch mandated that GE adopt Six Sigma as a business system. (Six Sigma is a business philosophy that espouses reducing variation in processes. This translates many times into substantial cost-savings.) Jack personally led Six Sigma. He hired and promoted people on the basis of furthering the Six Sigma banner. He fired those who resisted the new way of doing business. Thousands of people went through Six Sigma training. He brought in hundreds of ex-military to uniformly implement transformation enterprise-wide.

The CEO-led business transformation is well known and many companies have used the above playbook, sometimes well and sometimes poorly.

What happens when the CEO is not personally leading transformation? In my company, ADC, our CEO was interested in mergers and acquisitions. At company-wide forums he was scripted to say the right things about transformational initiatives but most people deduced his heart was not in it.

How do you lead change when the guy at the top is not leading it? There aren't many playbooks out there for doing this bottom-up. This book is one such playbook. It is a story of a small team within a large corporation that introduced a new way of serving customers and in a very short time, brought about business and cultural transformation.

We didn't chase shareholder value. We simply wanted to improve the customer experience and Sales' ability to close deals. What resulted was an explosion in shareholder value creation. In less than one year, we improved profit by millions of dollars, reduced inventory by millions, reduced lead times from 50 to 14 days, and reduced expediting over 90%.

How do you change from the bottom-up? If you are a frustrated transformation agent, this story is for you…

Chapter One

Why the need for transformation?

"What got you here won't get you there" quips Marshall Goldsmith. Such an appropriate phrase describes the dilemma faced by individuals, companies, even societies. In the 21st Century, change is happening at such breakneck speeds that people feel a sense of dislocation, uncertainty, even isolation. Technological breakthroughs are at the heart of such dislocations. Ever since companies like Intel produced new generations of microprocessors that continue to push the laws of physics, societies are struggling to cope with the repercussions of the speed of technological change. I mean, even my 75-year old dad is on Facebook. Those with the foresight to capitalize on the implications of hyper-speed-technology-induced-change have ridden to greater fortune, while others have stubbornly clung to yesterday's models and have quickly found their businesses obsolete.

Consider names that used to be famous: Netscape, America Online, even Yahoo. Not even a decade has passed and these companies no longer command the strategic dominance they once possessed in the Internet space. Or consider even a legendary company like Dell. Lauded for years by nearly every pundit, scholar, and consultant for their ingenious direct business model, Dell has recently opted to push their products through traditional distribution outlets like Walmart. Dell's languishing stock price and business demonstrates that even nearly invincible companies must continually change and even when they wholeheartedly recognize this, many times they cannot do so successfully.

The company currently all the rage in the free press is Apple. Steve Jobs' return to Apple in the late '90s heralded perhaps the most storied comeback in business history. With roots in personal computing, Apple has successfully branched out into music distribution, phones, and tablets. Their success story punctuates the point that those with the prescience to understand how to capitalize on the implications of societal and technological change will reap the rewards.

The need to change is so clear, the cautionary tales of failures and the legends of successes are so apparent, yet companies by and large find great difficulty in transforming themselves.

This book is about ADC, one such company that struggled to renew itself for years, until one team became the catalyst for making the transformational leap. Like many of these stories, ADC experienced great success at one point in its history. In the '90s ADC was a high-flying stock. ADC manufactured copper-based telecom equipment and enjoyed fantastic margins, upwards of 60% gross margins. ADC customized products to every whim and fancy of their customers and delivered products "yesterday." They could accomplish this because they were vertically integrated (meaning most manufacturing happened under one roof) and only had to deal with a few hundred suppliers. Customers rewarded ADC with 80% market share of their particular market niche. With a $400+ share price, the stock was so strong that people told me Cisco Systems was at one point on their acquisition target list!

Then the telecom bubble burst in the early 2000's. ADC's stock price plummeted to low single digits. ADC went from binging on acquisitions to shedding almost all of the acquisitions as quickly as possible. The company was on life support but the executive team managed to keep the company alive by focusing on the core business. Slowly, ADC began to rebuild itself.

The telecom world continued to change. Customers like AT&T and Verizon consolidated the North American telecommunications service provider industry. With this consolidation customers mercilessly drove supplier prices down.

With no pricing power, new products from ADC priced at 30% (or less) gross margins. Customers wanted the same level of service and customization for new fiber-optic as well as copper-based products. ADC gladly obliged. A dramatic drop in gross margins is a clear signal for a business model change, yet the culture clung to an "anything for the customer mentality." They attempted to fix the margin problem through both scale acquisitions and pursuing aggressive cost reductions.

To attempt to gain scale, ADC pursued acquisitions. ADC expanded into adjacent markets, entered the Enterprise market, and expanded into Europe, the Middle East, Africa, and Asia. From barely surviving at $400M of revenue, ADC grew again into a $1.5B company. It seemed that the scaling-up strategy was working.

However, these acquisitions combined with the "anything for the customer" culture resulted in a Gordian knot of complexity: portfolio proliferation, supply chain complexity, and order management complexity. We were basically chasing low cost for direct materials and direct labor all over the world.

For example, to keep up with customer-driven pricing pressures, they continued to move manufacturing to low-cost locations such as China. To lower component costs, ADC's supply chain grew from several hundred to several thousand suppliers around the world. Because we continued to offer the same level of service and customization, ADC started to air freight materials all over the world to hit delivery dates. The complexity became crushing as margins continued to drop, competition (now global) continued to escalate, and customers continued to relentlessly push for lower prices. ADC's stock price remained stagnant.

The need for change was obvious to management. They decided to aggressively transform the company...

Chapter Two

How to absolutely fail in leading a transformation

Management knew transformation was necessary to the survival of the company. And so they brought in consultants.

Many times the need for change is overwhelming, but what to do? Where to go? As business models become obsolete, with no apparent roadmap, many company executives turn to strategy consultants to help navigate the change. Management consultancies command huge premiums for their advice as executives ask them to simplify the complexity and point their business in the right direction. However, sometimes when top management asks for advice, they subtly abdicate personal responsibility for leading change.

How does this abdication occur? Whenever you see consultants' names appearing on charts as leaders of a transformation project, this might be an early warning sign of impending disaster. Or, if management simply rehashes a consultant's "playbook," they might subtly and unconsciously distance themselves from owning the playbook. Anytime something is important enough to spend millions of dollars on it, but not important enough for leaders to personally lead it, this signals to employees that the initiative is doomed to fail.

As a positive, consultants bring fresh eyes to problems and bring best practices from across industries. They hire the smartest minds and often simplify complex problems into easy to understand frameworks. On the negative side, many consultants interview their clients and produce thick binders of materials summarizing what they heard. This is the equivalent of asking the clients to show them their watch and then telling their clients what time it is.

In ADC's case, the company spent millions of dollars asking consultants to architect a new business model to handle portfolio complexity, supply chain complexity, and lead time complexity.

After months and months of analysis, the consultants produced reams and reams of presentation material with a blueprint for change. We called it "VECTOR" (Very Expense Corporate Total Overhaul... Really). Top management agreed with the recommendations and assigned teams to initiate transformation. We had initiative leaders, scorecards, metrics, and a whole host of people assigned part-time to the initiative. After several months, it became apparent that no transformation was occurring. The excuses were all the same:

> "I can't start my initiative until the other initiative is complete."

> "My project has so many interdependencies on other projects that if *they* [the ever present but faceless 'they'] don't get their deliverables complete, there's no way my project will be successful."

> "This initiative is getting in the way of real-work that needs to get done."

> "When Sales hears about this, they are going to puke all over it (which they did)."

> "We don't have enough resources."

> "We don't have enough analysis."

> "Our systems suck and I don't trust any of the data."

> "People's performance goals and incentives aren't aligned."

After a year of non-progress, we simply stopped reporting on project status, one project after another.

And then, "Hallelujah!" The company had to focus on shipping product to meet quarterly and year-end targets. "All hands on board, we've got to hit our revenue objectives! All these silly initiatives need to get dropped." And they did. The company thrived on crisis management and fire fighting. It was always easier to focus people on meeting revenue objectives than on changing the DNA of the company.

After the crisis passed top management noticed that the engine was still broke. Hmm, we just spent millions on the first initiative with no results. How about we rebrand it? Let's change the name and spend a few million more on consultants! This time, let's call it "DDT" (Doomed and Dead Transformation). While the title of the movie changed, the script was the same, and the people on the front lines knew it.

Last time the employees didn't experience any results from the project. So this time, the CEO would report all the savings resulting from the new initiative. The CEO would stand up at a town hall and announce "We saved the company $X million dollars as the result of our transformation." When it came time for the town hall, people were chuckling behind the scenes and mocking the announcement. The cost savings were the result of purchase-price savings from suppliers or engineering cost reductions, both of which the company did as normal course of business. Everyone could see the quick fake. Fundamentally, no behaviors changed, no processes changed in a transformative manner. The only observable behaviors were infighting.

Again, meeting revenue targets turned into the "all-hands on deck" crisis. The organization scrambled and dropped working on transformation. ADC stopped reporting on transformation projects. The crisis passed and still no transformation.

Millions of dollars in consultant fees, a new leader, a new program management office and yet a third incarnation of transformation began. Cynicism in the organization was rampant. "Here comes another flavor of the month initiative!" People just waited for this initiative to go away. So, this time around the CEO was getting a little incensed. "I hear there are blockers out there. If I find out who they are, I will fire them!" Word spread quickly. Don't be a blocker. Everyone feigned compliance and no blockers emerged.

And still nothing changed. Until, Hallelujah! Another crisis! "We have to ship product, book revenue and we can't be wasting time on these stupid initiatives." Heroics, mad frantic behavior, dialing for dollars, and pulling in orders until, "Yes, we hit our revenue targets!" Transformation? People learned to wait until the corporate initiatives went away. Invariably, they did.

Not too long thereafter the global economy experienced the Great Recession. Budgets got slashed and the program management office for transformation became the next casualty of war on the road to change.

So what happened? How do large-scale transformations fail? I'll give you five things not to do.

#1: Don't Boil the Ocean

Unfortunately, with large-scale transformations, the initiatives end up collapsing underneath their own weight. I call it the World War I strategy. Everyone get in line along a massive front and start pushing. Attempt to change everything, all at once. Just like trench warfare during World War I, progress becomes glacial, if non-existent.

Interestingly enough, with so many large scale failures you might think that the second, third, fourth time around someone would change the script. But no, each time in our case the successive leader would chart the same course of action. This should remind all of us of Einstein's famous dictum: "The definition of insanity is doing the same thing over and over and expecting a different result."

The first key takeaway is this: Don't boil the ocean, or as my friend likes to say "Don't make your goal 'world peace'."

Why does this pattern repeat itself? Part of the reason comes from ambitious financial targets top management lays out. "We want to save $100M in three years," the CEO or CFO might proclaim. The person responsible for transformation does the math and stacks up all the projects with their expected returns on investment, sketches out a high-level timeline and concludes, "in order to hit those numbers we have to do all twenty of these projects, NOW." However, the only projects that have an immediate payback are layoffs, product transfers to low-cost regions, engineering cost reductions, and supplier purchase price reductions. None of the aforementioned equals transformation.

The problem with transforming a business model is that it entails totally changing processes, behaviors, and systems, none of which are guaranteed to have an immediate return on investment. Sometimes there is a lag between when the new behaviors are instituted and when the resulting productivity equates to measurable cost savings. Most executives are not patient enough to wait. So, they attempt to execute transformation in a sweeping fashion and overwhelm employees to the point of inaction.

#2: Don't Let the Message Get Diluted

Secondly, the initiatives cascaded from top to bottom. There's nothing wrong with cascading initiatives down to the project level. Cascading represents best practice in deploying a strategy. However, the level of ownership felt and clarity of messaging communicated continued to wane as the cascading occurred.

Each time the messages went from the highest levels to the next level, the messaging got diluted. By the time the messaging reached the lowest levels, no one understood what was being communicated. All the lower level employees heard was that someone was trying to massively change the entire company. How that affected people on an individual level, no one could say. It just sounded threatening. Since mid-level management felt little ownership, the messaging would sound something like, "I don't know why we're doing this. Corporate is telling us to do this project." The lack of ownership translated into diluted messaging, which translated into lack of engagement, which translated into half-hearted compliance, which translated into failure.

The bottom line is that people knew the CEO did not personally believe strongly in the transformation and hence all communications that cascaded stopped two layers below him.

#3: Don't load your people to 120% capacity

Very closely related to the first point of attempting to do too much was the resourcing plan. If you were to sit in an all-day briefing on initiative status, you would see the same names appearing. Basically, the same dozen people would be asked to lead or participate in four to six initiatives with an expected 10 - 25% of their time allocated accordingly. I've observed this phenomenon quite often not only in transformational initiatives but in regular engineering projects. Management plans people at 120% of their capacity.

The assumption behind this planning is that everything must execute with military precision and every deliverable must be hit precisely on schedule. Has anyone ever heard of Murphy's Law? Murphy's Law basically states, "Anything that can go wrong will go wrong." For engineers or project managers this means your project will be more expensive and take longer than what that pretty Gantt chart is showing.

Although this phenomenon is well known, managers are at fault for accepting this level of resource loading. Why do they accept such unrealism? Remember what I wrote about those $100M objectives placed on everyone by the CEO or CFO? People may know that the goals are unrealistic, but very few people want to be labeled as "Mr. Can't Do." Better to salute with three bags full and then blame failure on the economy, "headwinds," customers, the strike in France, the War in Iraq…you get the picture.

Management is to blame for this overloading and so are the individuals named on each of these initiatives. There is a perverse sense of pride in being named on six initiatives. Yes these capable workers will gripe and complain about being loaded at 15% across 10 projects, but very few will really push hard to force their managers for a reasonable capacity loading.

Perhaps the majority of us have an over-inflated sense of ego that we unrealistically believe we can multi-task across so many projects. Or, maybe we are conflict averse and do not want to say "no." Just like management, better to say "yes" and just allow the project to fail. Blame the failure on management, on the economy, on customers…you get the picture.

#4: Don't treat project management as an 'Excel' exercise

A fourth major reason why transformational initiatives fail is because of the poor choice in selecting the project leader. Basic project management is a core skill. Initiatives ultimately fail or succeed due to the failure or success of their underlying projects.

When I joined ADC over five years ago, I was horrified at how the organization selected and treated project managers. I will try to say this as delicately as possible: in many of the projects I was associated with, the "project manager" was a glorified admin assistant who updated an Excel spreadsheet. No one paid attention to him or her. People who were assigned action items routinely moved out their dates and the "project manager" merely crossed off the previous date and updated the spreadsheet with a new "projected date."

As the "project manager" asked for reasons why certain date deliverables were slipping, I heard the same excuses at the project level that I heard at the initiative level.

"My action has so many interdependencies."

"I'm waiting for so-and-so to finish his action item."

"I can't start my action until such-and-such analysis is done."

Many times a whole host of people were invited to project meetings who were merely vaguely associated with the project. I constantly wondered, "What the heck are all these people doing at this meeting?" Perhaps people enjoy being invited to meetings, but very few people exhibited any sense of ownership.

Even worse, sitting around the room people would "volunteer" other people to complete an action item without that person's knowledge. This happened to me personally several times where I would find out a day before a certain due date that my name was on some Excel spreadsheet with an action item attached to it.

Does this sound like project management to you?

Project Management, Army Style

In the Army we had a saying that wars were won or lost at the platoon-level. In other words, generals are busy moving units on maps but squads and platoons do all the fighting. The U.S. military places a tremendous amount of institutional energy in developing their small unit leaders, particularly the non-commissioned officers. If you ever watch the television mini-series "Band of Brothers" you can see in graphic detail how small unit leadership translated into gains at the strategic level. Watch in particular the episodes on the Battle of Bastogne. A general drives around and exhorts the men to "hold the line." But you see in scene after scene the sergeants walking the front lines in the cold, redistributing ammunition, keeping the soldiers' morale up, and concentrating their squad's firepower at key points of the battle. This is the equivalent of good project management.

In my observation, one of the worst backhanded compliments is to say that someone is "tactical." The word tactical has implications that the person is narrow-minded, can't see the forest for the trees, and can only do what is in front of her. We like the word "strategic." However, good strategy is only as good as our ability to execute. Napoleon *strategically* controlled the battlefield because his troops *tactically* could march further and faster than opposing armies. America has more strategic options at fighting terrorists because we tactically can execute missions with special operations forces with high precision.

Let's not demean the role of good project management. The essential blocking and tackling of any large scale transformation is project management.

#5: Don't let a committee run things

Management by committee is one of the worst sins of modern corporate culture. Part of the reason why corporations create committees is due to the complexity of managing large, global operations. You can organize by country, by region, by business unit, by function, and by customer. Actions experienced in one silo create ripples in another. How do modern corporations cope with this complexity? Committees.

A perverse outcome of committees is the dilution of responsibility. With the complex repercussions associated with large transformations, very few people want the buck to stop at their name. So, the committee "decides" or more appropriately, does not decide matters.

Having served as the Director of Strategy, I participated in many committees. Because making decisions was difficult, we spent our time on very worthy endeavors of executive time, like naming initiatives. We would take up to six months revising names from "Global Reduction in Strategic Locations" (GRISL) to more positive sounding names like "Simplification of Total Unneeded Footprint" (STUF). (I've obviously changed the names to protect the innocent.)

Because so many committees consist of high-level executives, just getting these committees together even once per month took an act of God. The hurried executives would get briefed on project updates and because the executives were not close to the action, many would invariably say "we need more analysis."

Why don't these executives delegate more power and responsibility to people who are on the front lines? Good question. My guess is that when your career depends on the actions of others, you want to be darn certain that those actions won't bite you in the butt. This means that the executive needs to spend more time understanding the issue, but she doesn't have time because she has to catch a flight. Let's postpone the decision till next month when we can meet. Oh, we can't meet because two executives are too busy. Let's meet in two months to discuss. Were we supposed to make a decision? We need more analysis. You get the picture.

I've probably exhausted this topic on how to fail, but it is important to go through this shared pain together. Good decision-making results from experience and experience results from making bad decisions. Wouldn't you rather learn from other people's mistakes?

Chapter Three

Focus on the Critical Few (vs. the Trivial Many)

A VP of sales named John was ticked off. He decided to express himself at the annual global sales meeting: "If operations would just ship product on time, we'd have more sales." Heads nodded in approval. The salespeople felt like the operations group was purposely sabotaging them. John was on a righteous crusade to fix lead times, so he met with Bill, the new VP of Operations, privately....

When Bill joined ADC as VP of Operations, he was itching to take the role. As a seasoned VP of global operations, he had successfully implemented Lean Sigma in several large businesses. Unassuming, humble, and self-effacing, most people upon meeting Bill sensed there was something hidden under the surface of his friendly Midwestern demeanor. It was as if Bill had spent the last ten years memorizing Sun Tzu's *Art of War*.

In short, Bill unnerved many people. They knew underneath his genial exterior was an operations man who was hard as rocks. He was like a Prussian general who concealed his riding stick. After Bill interviewed for a job as VP of Operations, he thought to himself, "Wow, there's a lot of low hanging fruit. It'll be like picking up watermelons."

But Bill, unlike many of his change agent predecessors, understood the environment in which he operated. Many months later he told me, "You can coerce change. That is possible. If you're the CEO and you have absolute power, you can force people to change." He knew at ADC this was not the case. The CEO wanted transformation but by DNA was a deal-guy and loved to spend his time on acquisitions. So when it came time for the company to rally around the corporate transformation initiatives, Bill knew that the CEO would not put his personal capital on the line.

Acknowledging this, Bill knew he had to start small, build credibility, and generate momentum. Since he had a global manufacturing operation to run, he needed someone full-time dedicated to helping him drive change. Enter Shiv Venkataramani.

Shiv Venkataramani is a proud Brahman from Chennai, India. People who meet Shiv for the first time are impressed by his confidence, knowledge and arrogance. He studied at University of Massachusetts and obtained a PhD in chemical engineering. After several years at 3M as a Lean Sigma Master Black Belt, Shiv worked for a short time as an independent consultant for Select Comfort. One of the few Black Belts who actually understood both Lean and Six Sigma, Shiv did not tolerate fools gladly. Like a six-year old child, he grilled managers with his favorite question, "Why?" Managers who would answer Shiv with some trite phrase about how they had been "in the business" for 20 years would receive a verbal tongue-lashing of all the reasons their assumptions about what drove the business did not hold true. Shiv may have not fully understood their business but he knew something they did not, statistics.

Shiv mastered the art of applied statistics and could cut through the dense fog of obfuscation that different "experts" laid in front of him. Shiv understood concepts like process variation, normal curves, and confidence intervals that essentially enabled him to tear apart industry experts. "Your process is $%&#! You have a Cpk of -0.02 and you're telling me that by doing 'X,Y, Z' you are able to manipulate the results. What you are experiencing is Brownian motion where the results move in a chaotic fashion. If you plot your data on an SPC chart you would see that everything you're describing is within normal process variation and is not due to special causes!"

My wife and I love watching the movie *The Princess Bride*. If you recall one famous quote: "Never go in against a Sicilian when death is on the line!" I changed the quote to "Never go in against Shiv in a battle of wits." Shiv ended up becoming our secret weapon for transformation. He wielded both an intellectual scalpel and hammer and either sliced or bludgeoned his opponents verbally, depending on how he felt that day.

Shiv understood the need for small wins. So he slowly set about teaching Lean Sigma to a handful of "evangelists" who later became the company's green belts and black belts.

In the first year of the Lean Sigma program, Bill and Shiv oversaw modest improvements and gains. They did not attempt to radically overturn the culture by introducing another change management fad. However, they scored an important win with the customer in improving the manufacturing output for a product called *Rapid Fiber*. ADC's largest customer, Verizon, was ordering hundreds of units, but ADC could only supply a fraction of their demand. With Verizon's procurement team breathing down our necks, Shiv acted quickly. He mobilized two green belts to radically change their manufacturing process. Even after shutting down the manufacturing line for one week, they were able to double output and satisfy Verizon's demand. Crisis averted. More importantly, this win gave Bill and Shiv the credibility they needed to grow their Lean Sigma program.

I was one of the new disciples of Lean Sigma after watching a showcase where Shiv detailed the *Rapid Fiber* story to hundreds of managers. At the time, I was the director of corporate strategy. After Shiv's presentation, I went to him and asked if I could become a green belt. He agreed and we worked on a project together.

It was not long after I completed my green belt project that we fast-forward to the private meeting where John, the Sales VP, cornered Bill. This meeting has since become a bit of urban legend within the company. John is a 250 lb. Irishman, who can drink pints of Guinness for hours on end. (I saw him down 10 pints in one sitting, no joke). Towering above Bill, John lit into him. "My guys are spending hours just chasing down orders and delivery dates! Why can't we ship on time?" On and on he recounted all the times he felt burned by operations' inability to ship product.

The urban legend part comes from Bill's response. In his office, Bill sits on a Pilates ball with his shoes off. He brings his lunch every day in a Coleman cooler and eats apples and hard-boiled eggs sitting on his Pilates ball. And so, as John vented his anger, Bill sat there, chewing an apple, with his shoes off, sitting on his Pilates ball. "Is that all?" Bill asked. John wasn't and lit into him again. Another 15 minutes went by.

Finally, John completed his rant and Bill smiled and said, "I'd be happy to help you." This totally disarmed John, who was expecting fisticuffs. No, Bill executed non-defensiveness like a judo move. He quietly nodded his head. "You're right," he said. "Delivery is not where it should be. And I'm happy to do something about it. But I can't fix delivery on 80,000 part numbers. How about we focus on the 20% of parts that generate 80% of revenue?" John agreed.

The next week Bill called me into his office. "Young man, how would you like to work in Operations?" At the time I was getting tired of being a corporate Power Point jockey and was longing to get back to the front lines. "Bill, I would love it." "Great, you'll be in charge of aligning Operations and Supply Chain in support of Pull Replenishment. Shiv will work with you on

22

implementing Pull Replenishment." Scarcely six months ago I could barely spell 'Lean' and now Bill put me in charge of one of the most important Lean projects in the company.

Over the next year, Shiv and I worked with dozens of talented team members implementing Pull Replenishment. But, instead of making the same mistakes we saw in previous initiatives, we decided to do something novel. We decided to start small.

What in the world is "Pull Replenishment?" "Pull Replenishment" is a term that might be better stated as "build-to-order" (BTO). This is in contrast to "build-to-stock" (BTS). In a BTS world, schedulers "guess" what products they think customers will buy by looking at the previous 12-months of shipments. This is the equivalent of driving using the rearview mirror. Now if you are a retailer like Wal-Mart, stocking your shelves each year follows fairly consistent consumer demand patterns. And besides, many suppliers consign their inventory, leaving little risk for Wal-Mart. But at ADC, with 80,000 catalog numbers that were mostly custom configured for each customer, looking in the rearview mirror did not help forecasting finished stock. Why? 50% of our product mix changed each year. In other words, we were constantly building the wrong stock.

Pull Replenishment solves this by creating a build-to-order model only on the high-runners that have consistent volume year after year. But instead of guessing customer demand and building stock to match, in Pull Replenishment the operations group stocks component inventory and builds the final product only after receiving a real customer order. That component inventory is "replenished" when it falls below a certain level.)

Why start small? Starting small helps to reduce the "fight or flight" syndrome that large-scale implementations engender. I knew that implementing Pull Replenishment would be nothing short of a culture shift. Our culture had created massive complexity with an unsustainable build-to-stock system. Pull Replenishment could represent a threat to "how we have always done things around here."

Defining the Problem

For example, with over 80,000 catalog numbers, we were experts at proliferating products. On top of that, our sales force tended to quote unreasonable lead times to customers. Imagine going to a car dealer. The salesperson shows you a standard car with silver paint. He quotes you a price of $20,000. You say, "I'll take it, but I want it in purple with custom chrome trim, a spoiler, and tinted windows." He says, "no problem, when do you want it?" You say "tomorrow" to which he replies "no problem, anything for a customer." When you ask for the price, he says "$20,000." Because price and lead-time are not differentiated, the customer always chooses the more custom model. Once the order books the entire supply chain and operations is scrambling. "Purple? We don't even have purple paint. Custom chrome trim? We've never made the car with those before." More or less, that was exactly the predicament we were in.

In the '90s this business model worked. Like I wrote previously, ADC was highly vertically integrated, meaning most of the manufacturing occurred under one roof. As customers grew more powerful and demanding, management continued to explode the supply chain chasing lower cost labor and materials. In the past we could quote to the customer a lead time of "7 days" and then yell across the hall to the manufacturing group who could turn new products around quickly. But, when your supply chain explodes around the world, you may quote "7 days" but your Chinese supplier is quoting you "60 days" on components. Because our business model of "anything for the customer, now" never changed, we were airfreighting components from China. That's not exactly low cost.

Product proliferation created portfolio complexity, which in turn created supply chain complexity, which in turn created order management complexity. Our team was tasked to cut through this complexity to simplify our interactions with our customers and improve our delivery.

Defining what problem you are trying to solve sounds so intuitive and yet so many unsuccessful projects fail to do just that. Defining the problem is very hard. What *exactly* are we trying to solve? In our case we knew very simply that we wanted to improve delivery but when we dove into the details several questions arose: are we trying to improve our ship-to-promise performance? Are we trying to improve our ship-to-request performance? In a later chapter on metrics, I will go deeper into the thorny topic of choosing useful metrics. At the end of the day we chose an objective standard. Can we beat a market lead-time of 14 days? This was the problem we chose to solve.

Map the Process End-to-End

How can you get to where you want to go if you don't know where you are? I remember when I learned how to navigate using a map and a compass. The first task was to find out your location on a map with the corresponding 8-digit coordinate. Once I was tested for night land navigation and I plotted the wrong starting point. Not surprisingly, every point I went to was wrong, because my starting point was wrong. After failing the first go around, I spent more time ensuring I accurately plotted my points on the map. Using Lean techniques our team decided to map our order management process as it "really was" and thus find our true starting point.

On a cold wintry day, I gathered people from Sales, Product Management, Operations, Supply Chain, Customer Service, and IT to map out how we processed orders. After four days and hundreds of Post-it notes, we produced a 12-ft by 8-ft mural depicting the Herculean effort required by dozens of people to process and ship a simple order.

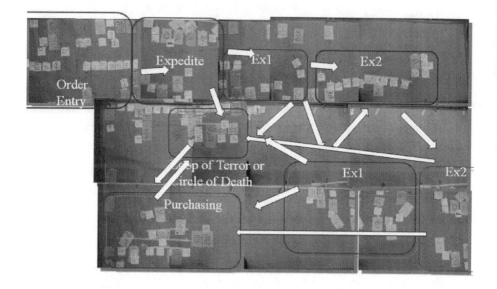

After we completed the process map, we stared at it as if we were staring into an abyss. The most common phrase uttered was "Oh my God! We do THAT?" In over 20 years, no one had ever mapped out end-to-end what the order management process looked like.

I admit, I felt a bit panicked that week looking at the part of the process map called the "circle of death." This affectionate phrase described the negotiation process between customers, Customer Service, Operations, Supply Chain, and suppliers in trying to improve lead-time dates. A daily back-and-forth of emails and phone calls greeted everyone who touched an order from the moment they arrived to work till they left exhausted for home. The circle of death was a round robin of "What do we have to do to improve the date? Do we need to airfreight components? Do we need to schedule overtime? Do we need more capacity?" The Pull

Replenishment initiative I was to lead would have to break the "circle of death."

Scope for Success

After whispering silently a few prayers, like, "Dear God, don't let me fail!" I gathered the team together and announced that if we were going to be successful, we would have to scope the project for success. We decided to pilot 36 part numbers from one product line using Pull Replenishment. I had seen previous initiatives grind to a halt trying to do too much at once. Furthermore, I thought of Einstein's quote about insanity many times. I may be dumb, but I'm not stupid. So while many thought our goals too modest, we agreed that we needed a small win to prove out the concept before implementing further.

It does not take a wise man to look at failure and choose a different course of action. This team decided to scope the first project for success. In a later chapter, I will go into more detail about how we achieved successful results, but it is important to note that without the initial scoping, we would have met with the same stagnation and inertia of previous initiatives.

There is a saying that "complexity kills." In our case it meant "complexity kills momentum." We could barely wrap our arms around the complexity of merely shipping an order. In order to tackle the problem, we reduced the scope of the problem to a manageable size.

Scoping for success is really the flip side of saying, "Don't boil the ocean." Whether it's losing weight, applying to college, or learning a new skill, we can greatly enhance our probabilities of success by scoping our endeavor to a manageable size. Success is like emotional oxygen. Without some degree of achieving a goal, we become quickly demotivated and give up.

Focus on the critical few

The theme of focusing on those critical few things that significantly "move the ball forward" continually reveals itself as a key to success. Akin to boiling the ocean, managers are often tempted to drown themselves in the minutiae of detail, poring over spreadsheets, Power Point presentations, monitoring dozens of key performance indicators (KPIs) on dashboards and thus ironically, dilute their ability to influence outcomes. The ability to focus on the critical few allows leaders to stay above the daily turbulence and direct resources where they will make the most difference.

What do we mean when we say "critical few?" This phrase is really an everyman's way of referring to the Pareto-principle. The Pareto-principle states that 20% of your customers, products, people, geographies, etc., contribute 80% of your profit. While the actual breakdown (80/20, 90/10) may vary depending on the circumstance, this principle is so prevalent in life that it becomes a distinguishing differentiator between those who are effective and those who are not.

When we started our initiative, Bill took his first cut at managing complexity. "I can't solve lead time problems on 80,000 SKUs. You might as well fire me if that's what you want," he said. Further analysis revealed some startling information: in any given year we did not sell 50,000 available SKUs but kept millions of dollars in inventory "just in case" someone called and asked for an order. This obsession with chasing revenue, any revenue, resulted in some interesting behaviors. Forget the fact that millions of dollars of cash were tied up in inventory; when we asked product managers why they kept so much inventory on the shelf they said "the lead time on components for these products is over 60 days. Customers won't wait that long for us to deliver and will go to a competitor. And many times the volume they order is 3x historical

demand. We have no way of predicting how much they will order."
Solution: throw inventory on the shelf for inventory that turns less
than one-time per year.

The next cut of data showed that in any given year, we sold
approximately 30,000 part numbers. Of those 30,000 parts, 15,000
in the "tail" of our Pareto curve represented only 1% of revenue.
Yes, and millions of dollars of inventory were stranded in that 1%
tail, turning less than one-time per year. The fear of losing $1 of
revenue, amassing tons of inventory in order to ship product
directly from stock led to some further interesting behaviors.

Since we had trained our customers that we were going to
absorb all the risk for demand volatility, customers were expecting
this "tail" (1% of revenue) to ship from stock in one day. We
stocked up, and if by chance they blew out our safety stock, we
were caught with a 60 to 90 day lead-time from our suppliers. This
infuriated the customers. One week they buy a product off the
shelf and the next week their order takes 90 days. Solution: lots of
yelling, screaming, airfreighting, emails, phone calls and executive
attention to pull in the supplier's lead time.

Even though this particular SKU was a custom application
with low overall annual volumes and sporadic demand, we stocked
the product like it was a daily purchase. After getting burned,
master schedulers increased the safety stock of inventory at
multiples of historic demand to avoid future pain. On the
manufacturing floor, operators learned to make extra, just in case.
Up and down the value chain, we buffered, hedged, and padded
inventory and schedules, just in case. No one wanted to get
burned.

And because this particular SKU was a custom application,
there was a high probability that in the next year there would be
zero-dollars of sales for this product. The 1% tail migrated into the

non-moving tail. We scrapped millions of dollars off our balance sheet every year but our delivery times never improved.

When we looked at the number of SKUs that comprised 80% of revenue, we found that only 3% of total available SKUs generated the vast majority of our revenue. Yet were the lead times on these items statistically any better than products in the tail? Oddly enough, the answer was 'No.' We had trained our customers to expect everything the next day. Because we stocked so much, occasionally the customer was lucky and got the product in less than one week. If they were unlucky, they had to wait many, many weeks. We calculated our 95% service level on high-runners to be 50 days. We averaged 16 days (a great reminder of the deceitfulness of using averages in statistics), but our standard deviation was also about 16 days.

Believe it or not, this always seems intuitive in hindsight, but all through the project we kept getting objections like "what about the other 60,000 part numbers? The customer will still be mad about our delivery performance on those." Shiv and I would listen and then reply, "Yes, but they will be ecstatic about our performance on the top 80%."

So, with Bill's guidance, we decided we were going to improve our lead times on parts representing 80% of volume from 50 days to 14 days. "What about the other 60,000 parts? What are you going to do to fix the other 60,000 parts?" "Nothing. It will be no worse than before."

And you know what? We were absolutely successful in focusing on the critical few. Rather than spending millions of dollars on consultants, software, new hires, and seeing no progress for years, we completed our initiative in 10 months. Now for those other 60,000 parts....

Chapter Four

Paint a picture of success

I once read a fable about a bunch of executives who sat around for hours debating mission statements. They debated how to perfectly word the statements from "We strive to *please* our customers," to "We strive for *exceptional* customer service." One said, "Statement #1 uses an active verb. Statement #2 sounds more passive." Another two hours of debate goes by. Another VP stands up and says, "Everything is about the customer. We don't have a business if we don't have customers. Let's say we do everything for the customer." Heads nodded. (You can't deny the logic.) So down came the pronouncement: "We are customer-centric. Everything we do is to make the customer happy."

When the sales organization received the mission statement they smiled. "It's about time people started talking about customers. We are so darn internal focused in this company." And that was a very true statement. Heads nodded. So when the most aggressive customers asked for 10% price decreases the sales people said, "Yes, Mr. Customer. We'll make up for it in volume."

The finance department and operations was horrified to hear about the price decrease. When they did the math they realized that volume would have to increase 40% just for profits to stay even with the 10% price decrease. They protested with sales but the VP of Sales held up a copy of the company mission statement and said, "You're fighting our core values. We'll make up for it in volume."

The next line of the mission statement stated, "We deliver the highest possible quality to our customers." The engineering department smiled. So when procurement, finance and operations came to engineering and told them that they needed to use more standardized parts the chief of engineers held up a copy of the vision and mission statement and said, "We're not a 'Hyundai.' We're more like 'Ferrari' so we're not going to use cheap parts in our works of art."

When the accounting dust all cleared, the company was producing products with 30% gross margins with a 35% operating expense. The math says that the company was generating a -5% operating income. This is what happens when vague mission statements trickle down to the masses without a clear understanding of the business model the company operates under.

The problem with mission statements

What so many of these mission statements lack is clarity, a "What does that mean for me?" kind of clarity. Companies seeking transformation need to help employees define success down to the behavioral level. It is not enough for senior management to come down from the mountain after strategic planning and communicate their epiphanies: "We will be a flat networked company vs. centralized. We will be nimble, not stodgy. We will tap into every employee's creativity to generate new innovations."

Those types of statements sound somewhat specific until an employee tests the waters. She reaches out to leaders in other business units and functions for her project and gets her hand slapped. "You need to clear it with me before you do something like this," her manager tells her. "Please copy me on all emails regarding your project. Oh, by the way, corporate is going to have training on the new flat-networked culture. I want to send you to it." The fact that companies daily live out double standards to their values and missions statements should surprise no one. The vibrant and passionate young lady goes to the very expensive training on "being a flat company" and decides that being a flat networked company is just not worth the pain. She will either succumb to the pressure and do what thousands of others do, put her head down, or she will leave.

A clear vision requires behavioral clarity. This means more than Power Point slides. When conducting different strategy surveys, we found that one of the top reasons why strategy did not translate into execution was that people could not articulate, "What does this mean for my job?" Without a personalization of the vision, people could not envision themselves as part of the vision.

How mapping the current state helps people visualize the problem

One of the first things we had to do was to translate what our current process looked like and felt like to people on the front lines, across multiple functions. In other words, most people dutifully fulfilled their portion of an enterprise-wide process and then threw their mess over the wall to the next function downstream in the process. An example of this was our order management *kaizen event*. A kaizen-event is a weeklong process improvement session, where people in a manufacturing or transactional setting take apart and stitch back together their processes. I was told that Customer Service had already "kaizen'd the process." What they had done was only focus on Customer Service's narrow part of the process. The result was that they created their version of an "easy button" to expedite orders. They threw the problem over the transom to the next function. That's the problem of using kaizen techniques solely within a silo of an enterprise process.

I wrote in a previous chapter how important it was to map the process. When we did this, you could see the collective light bulbs turning on. "This is what happens when I throw my mess over the wall!" People were surprised and a little horrified at the "circle of death" they had created. No one needed to convince anyone of the need to change. The participants created their own emotional leverage to change the process.

Writing a script of what success looks like

We then asked our team, "What would success look like if we break the circle of death?" We brainstormed over 60 ideas like:

"Give the best date first. Stop moving dates around."

"No expediting or escalations."

"Make sure all materials are available."

"Confirm a customer order with a delivery date within 24 hours."

Without even going into the Lean Sigma toolkit, the team was creating the template for how we would execute Pull Replenishment. Since they originated the ideas themselves, the team bypassed the usual resistance that the other corporate initiatives experienced.

We then formalized the improvement ideas by publishing a script of what a customer would experience in the new process. In our case, a) the customer would call for a quote; b) we would quote them our best lead time; c) the customer would give us an order; d) we would confirm the order with that best lead time within 24 hours; e) the sales order would generate a production order; f) operations would immediately begin building the order; g) operations would ship the order to the distribution center; h) the distribution center would ship the order on the date confirmed to the customer.

By clarifying what the end state would look like from a customer perspective, each function that touched any of these steps were then empowered to change their process to meet the end state. This translated into dozens of work streams, of which I was only conscious of half of them at any given time. Rather than dictate each work stream and drive hard deliverables for each, I told each work stream leader, "You know what success looks like. If I get run over by a bus you still know what to do."

It was simply amazing to see what people did with the freedom and trust they were given. People could envision the end state because they could see how their actions affected the entire process and more importantly, affected the customer experience. The vast majority of the customer complaints would be solved. And for a culture that thrived on pleasing the customer, this project gave them the motivation to drive toward completion.

So, rather than act like a taskmaster updating dashboards and Gantt charts, I acted more like a cheerleader encouraging the teams to fulfill their mission.

Help people visualize the change

In our case, we found that the change was less scary for people when we could help them visualize it. A young lady in HR gave us an idea: Why don't we demonstrate a pull system using ice cream sundaes? Brilliant! We would allow hundreds of people to interact with a pull system, live. And the benefits of their attendance would be an ice cream sundae.

We sent out an invitation to hundreds of people advertising the "free sundae." In manufacturing companies (and I suspect, in most others), the way to people's hearts is through their stomachs. The offer worked. We packed our cafeteria with several hundred workers. Bill took the first few minutes to talk them through the basics of a pull system…one-piece flow, operating to takt time, and visual management. Luckily, we had a counter-example of a non-pull system during our annual United Way campaign. We had a sundae line that took *forever* to get through. The line wasn't balanced, we had bottlenecks, and people stood there waiting while the ice cream melted.

This time, we set every part of the line to a two-second takt time. That means, every step of the line would take two seconds. Grab a bowl (2 seconds), step. Get your choice of topping (2 seconds), step. Put whip-cream on top (2 seconds), step. Receive a cherry on top (2 seconds), step. We advertised that we would serve 150 people in 5 minutes. Ready, go.

It worked exactly as advertised. People could see a massively efficient operation using a pull system, real-time. Bill acted as the *water spider,* busily refilling kanban bins so that the line never stopped. Finally, we showed what happened to a line when we received an expedited change order. The efficient line came to a crashing halt. We simulated the "circle of death" in the supply chain to get the unique component and how difficult it was to get the component to the manufacturing cell. In this case, we used a demand for crushed peanuts as our change order. Bill simulated yelling at the supply chain to expedite a pallet of crushed peanuts and then ran to the back of the warehouse to bring the expedited order to the line. It was a wonderfully amusing demonstrating of *disrupting flow.* The demonstration was a hit. We satisfied people's palates, and now had an object lesson to use as we continued our implementation.

Several months later, a black belt named Ali and I used the ice cream sundae demonstration as our template to implement continuous flow in our sheet metal operation. "Guys, remember the ice cream sundaes? Everything flowed from one step to another. How can we implement something like this?" The operators recommended using ANDON lights, lights with a red-yellow-green indicator, as a method of signaling to each other when their kanban bins were running empty. We trialed the kanban signaling and increased our output from our automated sheet metal shear 40%. This was all because people could visualize from the ice cream sundae demo and apply it to their own operation.

Walk people through the journey

People don't know what they are going to experience as they are going through change. It's important to walk them through. What are they going to feel? What are they going to see? How is the change going to impact them? The way Shiv and I handled this was to aggressively use media through our Internal Communications Department.

Our team tried every type of media possible. One of our team members brilliantly produced several videos after kaizen events, detailing the problems faced and improvements implemented. Shiv and I worked with the marketing department and produced a podcast series, walking people through the initiative. We held several ice cream sundae demonstrations to show live what a pull system looked like. And, I held several briefings to large stakeholder groups in advance of every project roll out.

The other aspect of walking people through the journey is to be honest about the risks. Will customers who previously asked us for shipments "yesterday" be happy when we stopped jumping through hoops and going through the circle of death? No. It will take time for behaviors to change. Would salespeople be happy that they could no longer be the heroes for the customer and order Operations to go into the circle of death? No. It would take time for behaviors to change. Will we fail 5% of the time? Yes, and sometimes we would fail badly. (Statistically, this has proven itself out).

However, in walking people through the journey we constantly stressed the positive benefits. Sales would not have egg on their face from orders being moved out to 100-day lead times. Sales would receive 50% of their time back. Customers would not have to pay contractors and installers to sit around waiting for materials. They could plan around a 14-day lead-time and their projects would be complete on time and on budget.

By not promising that Pull would make all their problems go away, people accepted the risks and we moved forward together, eyes wide open, arms locked together.

Manage by End State

In the U.S. military we have a term called "manage by end state." In this case, "manage by end state" comes from the German military term "Auftragstaktik." In creating *blitzkrieg* form of warfare during World War II, the German Wehrmacht had to teach their panzer commanders to think quickly, improvise, and to make decisions faster than their adversaries. In punching through an enemy's lines, these panzer units would often outrun their supply trains, overtake the enemy's rear lines, and outpace the ability of the headquarters to dictate to them their next set of orders. So instead, they were given general guidelines, like "Drive the British to Calais," as a superordinate set of orders on top of their immediate combat orders. This allowed the German army to defeat the British, French, and Poles in a matter of weeks.

The United States Army not too long after translated this into our own military doctrine, a combined arms doctrine. We saw evidence of this doctrine at work during Desert Storm, when

General Norman Schwarzkopf defeated the Iraqi military in 100 hours.

In the fog of war, the ability to command and control largely goes out the window. A commander must trust that his subordinate company commanders and platoon leaders understand "commander's intent." All operations orders are simply a fleshing out of commander's intent. Down to the squad leader level, officers and noncommissioned officers are taught that if the chain of command gets killed, they are to continue the mission and fulfill the commander's intent. For this reason among others, the U.S. military is the most adaptable, flexible, and competent fighting force in the world.

Similarly, dashboards, Power Point charts, and spreadsheets are often inadequate in managing a massive collective endeavor in the business world. Too many times, managers will spend half their time updating dashboards in preparing for management meetings. In doing so, management becomes isolated from the *gemba,* a Japanese term for "the place where the value is created."

It is only when everyone knows the mission, knows what "right looks like," that people can focus their time on actually improving the process versus updating spreadsheets (which, in Lean Sigma is more often than not *'muda,'* which in Japanese means 'waste.') In the gemba, leaders gain an intuitive sense of whether their people are getting closer to the end state or not. One day a VP from another company asked Bill what dashboards he used to get a sense of his people's performance. Bill replied "None. I just walk around. How about you?" The other VP replied that they had a set of dashboards and scorecards that were created by consultants.

When managers continually micromanage their people's work, they are implying that they know more than their own people. That impression won't motivate those they are trying to lead.

39

One reason why managers feel this need to give their own "expert" opinion on seemingly every subject is that their authority often exceeds their competency. This shouldn't surprise us, but it is understandable. When becoming a manager, most people are selected because they are strong individual contributors. Such new managers often confuse the skill set of management with individual achievement. Or in other words, they believe what got them their job is what will make them good management.

Nothing could be further from the truth. The definition of individual achievement is the effective and productive efforts of an individual in accomplishing a task. Good management is far different. It is the optimization of resources, time, talent, and treasure in accomplishing a series of tasks, missions, processes, or projects. Because a manager's authority is often greater than his competency, he sometimes makes up for his sense of inadequacy by trying to sound smarter than he really is in micromanaging his employees.

One remedy for this is management by end state. My advice to managers is to practice saying "I don't know; what do you think? How would you get there?" Or, I say "I need your help. It seems you have the right skill set for this." Many people are simply flattered to be asked their opinion. Asking for help empowers them to help you and in doing so activates their intrinsic motivations.

Managing by end state is one of the most powerful means of leading a large, diverse group. While management is the optimization of resources towards a specific goal, leadership is the envisioning and communicating of those goals. Leadership paints a picture where none previously existed. The clarity of the picture brings order to chaos. Confusion is the enemy. Leaders dispel confusion and unify efforts toward a common vision.

Chapter Five

Manage Stakeholders' Expectations
(and prevent management tampering!)

I don't know why change management is associated with HR. Well, yes, I do. Change management is about the soft side of leadership, something too many managers are uncomfortable with. *I want to do strategy, I want to set out plans, and then I just want things to happen.* Unfortunately, if the plans include people, you need change management.

Change management is the art of setting expectations, relieving fears, uncovering resistance, helping people envision the path, and motivating people to move. In a large scale project or business-transformation, change management is the single, most difficult undertaking.

Engaging Stakeholders

The first step to successful change management is to understand who will intersect with your project, both upstream and downstream. When you write out the list, you will find that the number of stakeholders is quite large. Start with functions: Sales, Customer Service, IT, Product Management, Master Scheduling, Supply Chain, etc. Next, write out specific people's names with influence in the organization. Then write whether they are for, against, or neutral to the project and why. Then write what you are going to do to help alleviate their concerns, or capitalize on their favor. Finally, review this list, memorize your plan, and then burn it. The last thing you need is for someone to see a spreadsheet with their name on it and with "neutralize this sucker" written next to their name.

Secondly, meet with these stakeholders one on one. Understand their pain points, their hopes, and their fears. They will signal to you where they naturally align either with or against your project. They will give you helpful tips on who else needs to be involved. As you meet with stakeholders elicit from them what success looks like from their perspective. I listen and then rephrase what I've just heard: "So you're saying if we can confirm a customer order within 24 hours versus the usual seven days you will be happy?" Understanding their definition of success helps a project leader craft the project plan and appropriately scope the deliverables of the project.

Third, in change management I try to increase every stakeholder's skin in the game. It's not enough that they voice their complaints. What I do is invite them to the table with the caveat, "You're invited but that means you're in the boat rowing too."

You think this is a lot of work? It is. How do you think legislation in the U.S. gets passed? It's all stakeholder analysis, lobbying, and change management. Unfortunately, unlike Congress, none of us have billion dollar pork-barrel chits to trade for votes. If you're going to start a movement from the bottom up, you have to use your creativity and hustle up support by talking to stakeholders one person at a time.

Managing Management

If you ever get tapped on the shoulder to manage a project that crosses multiple functions, turn and run the other way! No, in all seriousness, once you cross-organizational boundaries, the complexity of managing the project goes up exponentially. If you have to deal with high-level executives, be prepared for the "Pointy Haired Boss" effect (with homage to the Dilbert cartoon). Also be prepared for numerous people to show up out of the woodwork acting offended that they weren't consulted about your project.

If only the description above were an exaggeration! Many of us have experienced "death by committee." Couple that with many executives' desires to appear competent and constantly express their "expert opinion" on subjects they have no expertise in, is it any wonder that so many projects are over budget and late?

Here's where the Lean Sigma methodology actually helps quite a bit. Luckily, in the U.S., there are still so many managers and executives who barely understand Lean Sigma. This is both a blessing and a curse. On the curse side, so much good could be accomplished with more constancy of purpose at the top using Lean Sigma. But occasionally, ignorance is a blessing, especially when it comes to dealing with executive stakeholders.

Using the DMAIC process

Using the DMAIC process (Define, Measure, Analyze, Improve, and Control) in managing a project is a powerful way to solve difficult problems. In and of itself, DMAIC provides a robust problem-solving framework to hone in on variables (which we call 'critical x's) that significantly change the measured outcome (which we call the 'y-variable' or dependent variable). If you don't understand what I just wrote, then good! Chances are most executives don't either. Use that to your advantage.

If you're not managing your project using DMAIC, you might want to take a 2-week green belt course somewhere and learn the DMAIC methodology.

Here's why I've found it works in managing stakeholders. When I bring a group of stakeholders into a meeting, I will often walk through the DMAIC methodology as how I will manage the project. After about 5 minutes, the stakeholders have mentally determined, "This stuff sounds like Greek rocket-science. Better leave it to the experts."

Having seen so many large-scale transformation programs fail, I needed to keep my project, Pull Replenishment, from being taken over by a committee. So I launched the initiative and walked all the stakeholders from Sales, Operations, Customer Service, Product Management, and Supply Chain through the DMAIC methodology. In order to manage scope creep I said, "O.K., we are in the *define phase*. This is where we determine scope and objectives. Once we lock in on the project charter, we will not deviate till the project is complete. If we find there are further considerations, we can add them to a follow-on project, but we are following our DMAIC project charter."

In the beginning, I had this conversation it seemed daily. Our project started with very modest project goals and few were happy with what it would accomplish. This brings us to the second stakeholder management tool: the multi-generation project plan.

Multi-generation project planning

Because people tend to boil the ocean when initially starting an ambitious endeavor, they often fail to generate the necessary momentum to realize their goals and sustain progress. Breaking a large endeavor into a multi-generation plan is a powerful way to manage scope creep, stakeholder expectations, and create time and space to generate momentum.

How does it work? Really simple: you can in one simple Excel-spreadsheet map out a "crawl, walk, run" progression of projects that start with modest goals but create the necessary competencies and momentum to realize an ambitious vision. Here's the roadmap I laid out for my stakeholders:

Pull Replenishment Roadmap

	Wave 1	Wave 2	Wave 3
Goals	Put 36 part numbers from one product line on Pull	Increase # of product lines to 5 and increase number of SKU's to 200	Increase # of product lines to 18 and increase number of SKU's to 2,000, representing 50% of revenue
Competencies	Supply Chain enablement, lean manufacturing cell, order management	Supply Chain enablement, configure to order, BOM restructuring, line balancing	No expedite poke yoke, supplier performance monitoring, aligning kanban with SAP
Benefits	Prove the concept	Demonstrate scalability	Time as a Weapon

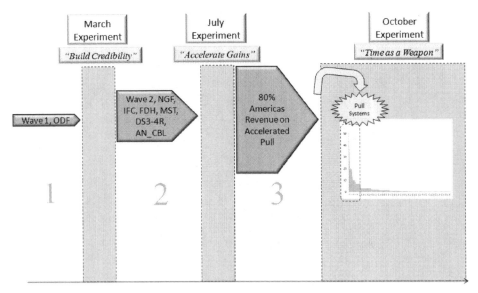

Exhibit A: Pull Replenishment Strategy Concept Sketch

As you can see, I use both words and pictures to convey the same message to different types of people: those who visualize concepts and those who don't. In either case, you have to convey the benefits that each successive project will bring. This is truly a case of delayed gratification. Executives tend to be impatient, so you have to show them that the journey will be worth the trip.

Multi-generation project planning will give you time and space to gain a foothold, generate momentum, and realize your ultimate vision. As a leader, it is your obligation to set your people up for success. In the beginning most people (though they won't say it) lack the confidence to take bold and aggressive actions. The multi-generational project approach works well to build that confidence through creating momentum.

Whenever I kick off something new, I try to elicit from the different players what their definition of success looks like. Not surprisingly, their words reveal that they are looking for the equivalent of "world peace" often expressed as, "I just want the problems to go away." At that point, I remind them, that the first project will be the equivalent of a lay-up. The gains will be modest. It will take 90-days to iron out the new process, but to be patient. Good, robust processes scale up quickly. If the stakeholders demonstrate they are patient enough, then I switch to project manager mode and focus on execution. In the beginning stages of a new initiative, execution means creating momentum.

Chapter Six

Create Momentum

Creating momentum is so vitally important to accomplishing your goals, that I cannot overstate it. Our entire initiative lived off momentum. Momentum is how we gained credibility with skeptics. Momentum is how we converted unbelievers. Momentum is how we carved out resources among competing priorities. Momentum is how we created visibility throughout the corporation. Once you identify the 'critical few' through using the Pareto-principle, your first question should be "how do I generate momentum?"

Momentum is kissing cousins to the quick win. However, I have seen many green belt projects completed with some tangible benefits that created absolutely no momentum. So, it may be instructive to distinguish between just picking low hanging fruit and genuinely creating momentum.

To give a few examples of quick wins that generated no momentum: You can do a simple cost reduction project. Hurray, great, what does that mean to the big picture? I've seen projects focused on training a certain number of people. The training was executed well, the curriculum was well developed, hundreds of people were trained, people complimented the quality of instruction, and then...nothing.

Or, a function improves their process in a silo. When I conducted my order management kaizen I was told "We've already *kaizen'd* order management to death." Yes, in your little silo, but the process touched almost every function in the company. The result of the previous kaizen was that they made it easy on themselves to throw their problem over the wall to the next function. That was a quick win with no momentum.

Or, I participated in a product rationalization initiative. Hurray! Finally! Reducing portfolio complexity is a well-known strategy used by turnaround artists and private equity specialists to generate shareholder value. We went through the analysis and eliminated 10,000 SKU's! Was there any bottom line impact? No, the only ones chosen were those that had zero dollars of sales in the last two years. Because of our product complexity, we eliminated stuff that no one was buying anyways. Worse, we maintained the ability for a customer to reactivate the SKU, which did happen. No momentum.

Or, you look around at all open projects, take credit for other activities and glob it all under your banner. I've seen this one happen in all sorts of ways. We did normal cost reductions every year. During one year, we labeled any cost saving effort "transformation." Yet, no behavior change had occurred. "Transformation indeed!" people harrumphed.

The flip side of this is when a strategic initiative is announced and every pet project gets relabeled under the banner of that initiative. It's the corporate equivalent of Congressional pork-barrel projects. Every Tom, Dick, and Harry wants to be a priority and have access to finite resources, so hey, we're part of "Strategic Initiative X" too! Just like boiling the ocean, resources get diluted over too many projects and the initiative dies, having created no momentum, no shareholder value.

Or, how about another software installation! If I had a dollar for every time people suggested software as the panacea to problems I could retire right now. Over the years, we spent millions of dollars on different software systems and successfully completed the project. No momentum, no transformation, no shareholder value created. Why? "Because no one's using the software;" "No one wants to use the software;" "It takes too much training to use the software;" "We only installed the basic set. To get full benefits, we'll have to install X-Y-Z upgrade and bolt-on." Along with hiring consultants, installing new software often proves itself to be a costly waste. No momentum, no transformation, no shareholder value created.

So these are some examples of doing projects that do not create momentum. How then, DO you create momentum?

Momentum comes from the collective excitement and positive emotions displayed by people when the name of your project is evoked. The essential sentiment that must be shared is, **"It's working!"** It is most important that your core team believe this, especially during water cooler moments or over a few drinks. Those moments reveal principally whether your project is destined for glory or heading to the dumpster. (I will share in a few chapters how to evoke these positive emotions at a kaizen event.).

The other important group of stakeholders is the people who touch the processes being transformed. I can't tell you how many Power Point presentations I've seen from executives boasting their projects are "green." Meanwhile, the troops are grousing about "what a waste of time" the initiative is. Does it then go without saying that most monthly management reviews are a costly waste of time? Lean philosophy espouses a view that ground truth is found "in the gemba." The gemba is the place where the value is created. Ironically, generally pay and rank is inversely proportional to the proximity of the gemba. Executives, who make the most, are the least in touch with the gemba. This applies not only to everyday business, but also at the project level.

Is it any wonder that most big projects are destined to fail? Those doing the work have little concept or clue that the initiative is even going on. They may hear about it at a big meeting, see posters here or there. But by and large, once you go two levels below the executive sponsor, all messaging gets diluted and all understanding of connection to strategy gets lost.

To create momentum, tie little steps to the big picture

So, the first key to creating momentum, even as you start with very small pilot projects is to never lose an opportunity to convey its connection to a strategic vision. People want to know where they fit in the big picture. They want to know how the first project will lead to something more substantial and yes, transformational.

Illustrations and word pictures work great to help people visualize the connection. One that I often use is an illustration about climbing mountains. I show five sets of mountains in progression: the Sierra Nevada foothills, the Scottish Highlands, the Appalachian Mountains, the Swiss Alps, and finally the Himalayas. "We are here," I say pointing to some foothills.

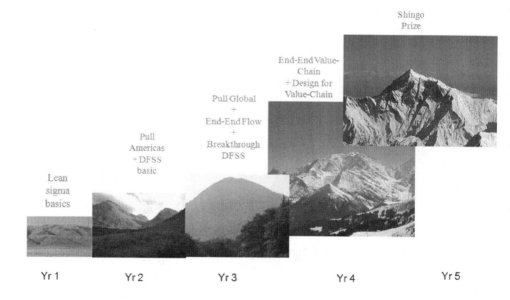

"O.K., it's not so great or fun tromping around in the foothills because our lungs aren't strong yet and our legs fatigue easily. We need to strengthen our back and limbs. This Lean project is like hiking around in the foothills. We are doing this so we can hike through some highlands and the view there is beautiful.

After that, the next set of projects will be like hiking the Appalachian Trail. That's Pull Replenishment. It's long, it's tough, but what a great experience! Once our basic skills are perfected, we might have to learn some new skills, or use technical equipment to climb the Alps. That's when we tackle *Pull in the Value-Chain*. Finally, our sight is set on the Himalayas. We may have to learn additional skills, use oxygen in thin air, but here is where we can rightly say we have mastered mountain climbing." At that point we will apply to win the Shingo Prize (Lean equivalent of The Baldridge Award for Quality).

I try to tie what we are doing today to a greater vision, something that is daunting, but inspirational. If I don't walk people through the journey, they usually look at the present with either boredom or disdain. In their minds the scope is never big enough to solve all the problems they want solved. But, because their aspirations are bigger than their competency, most fail executing. (See Chapter 2 on *How to Fail*).

So communicating how a project fits in relation to a greater strategic vision helps people understand how their contribution fits into a bigger picture, but that in of itself does not create momentum. No, in order to generate momentum, you have to create change, fast! The change must affect people who touch a process and the change must be perceived as better.

Those who have to live with the change must believe the resulting change creates more value for customers and that their life is better for it. That doesn't mean that there isn't *some* leverage applied on those reluctant to make the change. It just has to be done in a way that those who participate will agree in an unscripted moment, that the change was worth it.

To create momentum, change things, IMMEDIATELY

Our primary vehicle for executing rapid change was the kaizen event, imbedded in a Lean Sigma project. A kaizen event is a gathering of anywhere from 7 – 20 people (depending on how complex the process is) to transform a process, on the spot. Blending people who touch the process with a supervisor and a couple people who bring totally fresh eyes to the table is a necessary ingredient to a successful event.

Essentially, a kaizen event facilitator (a Green Belt or Black Belt) will conduct some on the job training about Lean principles or tools: value stream mapping, setup reductions, one-piece flow etc.., and then the team will walk the gemba. They will go and follow the process, step by step and ask questions. Why do we do things this way? After walking the process, many times the facilitator will consolidate observations on a process chart or value stream map, visually depicting the process end-to-end. People experience so many "aha moments" as they see bottlenecking at critical handoffs from one process step to another. Then, the facilitator asks the team to brainstorm ways of improving the process. The team comes up with the ideas.

Once the team comes up with solutions, the "magic" of the kaizen event happens. The team begins implementing some of the solutions immediately. Over the course of one week, the team attempts to implement as many solutions as possible. I've seen 33% to 60% productivity improvements in one week using this method. People finish the week exhausted, but elated at what they have accomplished.

The kaizen event wraps up with 30-day homework. What can the team get done in 30 days? The project leader follows up on the 30-day assignment. Usually, the kaizen event plus 30-day homework generates enough movement on those "critical X's," those variables that statistically demonstrate a process has improved that the Lean Sigma project can move to Control Phase. The Control Phase is part of the DMAIC process where an improvement is stabilized and turned into the standard operating procedure.

Embedding a kaizen event into a DMAIC project enables project managers to complete small, bite-sized projects in 90 days. And just like a new Congress or President tries to implement various programs or sign new legislation in their first 100 days, you essentially have 90-100 days to show some results before your initiative loses momentum. To create momentum, tie lots of little projects together

In my case, we had multiple small projects occurring simultaneously in Operations, Customer Service, and Supply Chain to accomplish my initiative-level first project. If you recall, we had chosen only 36 part numbers on which to test Pull Replenishment. We created three separate project work streams focused on 1) enabling our supply chain to deliver components in 14 days with a kanban replenishment method 2) enable one-piece flow at the manufacturing cell level and 3) implement a "no-expedite" process on the order management side so that we didn't create a bullwhip effect in moving around and expediting orders.

As those three work streams progressed, I decided that I would draw a line in the sand for a common deadline. We had to coordinate our movements because each work stream was interdependent on the others for success. So, I decided at a project meeting, "We have to have everything complete by February 28th. We are going to do a March Experiment where we will put all of our ideas to the test." As an aside, people are rarely motivated to complete a project without forced deadlines. In the beginning weeks of my project, each work stream leader kept pushing out his or he deadlines to April and May. Nope. We had to finish by the end of February or the whole project was going to fail.

To create momentum, force deadlines on the team

To my surprise, with a forced deadline, people scrambled and got their work done. We communicated broadly to our Executive Steering Committee that we were doing a March Experiment to pilot Pull Replenishment on a limited basis.

How do you force a deadline? Very simply, invite executives to a readout where you will have your people present their progress. Let your teammates do 80% of the briefing and give them all the credit during this very visible moment. Without deadlines people will constantly tell you that they don't have enough resources to complete their action items.

The March Experiment went off without a hitch. We advertised a 95% service level and achieved 97%. Better yet, we achieved this on-time delivery without breaking the back of the organization. What really excited people was the actual lead-time performance. We could ship products 95% of the time in 14 days vs. 50 days for the same service level. Although the pilot was modest in scope, we only shipped about $1M of product, it was substantial enough for everyone to see that we had broken through years of stagnation and had created momentum!

This momentum set the stage for further gains, of which we will explore in the next several chapters. I can state emphatically that the entire initiative ran on momentum. In previous grandiose initiatives, the failure to achieve a bonafide "win" ended up sapping the organization of energy. We would, literally, run out of steam. It would often take six months for an initiative to scope all the underlying projects and then go through a series of training to get people up to speed. By then, people were tired of going to the different training meetings, scoping meetings, steering committee meetings, and other pow-wows.

We saw that small wins connected with a larger vision gave people emotional oxygen. You could see their confidence level grow over time. Many started the project making very tentative statements like, "We'll see..." or, "I'll be interested to see if this thing is successful..." or, "I'll reserve judgment." They replaced their half-hearted, non-committal statements with statements like, "We're doing it...It's not a lot, but we're making progress..." and, "Let's keep this thing going...We've got something good." All of these statements are both honest and hopeful. While hope may not be considered a strategy, hope sustains the heart.

I knew that people in my company were jaded from high-flying rhetoric of past transformational initiatives. They were just waiting for the projects to end with a whimper so they could go back to doing the 'real work.' This time around we created momentum and injected optimism into the organization that was based on facts and reality.

In your project, think about what you can commit to in 100 days. Scope down your grand visions into something that you can achieve and build upon. Let me know if it works for you.

Chapter Seven

How to Use the Kaizen Event as an Accelerator

I already wrote about how important the kaizen event was in creating momentum, but there are enough specific details about how to set one up, that this deserves its own chapter. This chapter is for both Lean practitioners and novices. Even those who know nothing about Lean can facilitate a session that empowers people. If Lean Sigma talk scares you, go ahead and skip this chapter.

Physically walk the process

Physically walking a process is called a gemba walk. Try to be as thorough as possible. For our project we started out with how we quoted to our customers. We would often quote lead times such as "7-21 days." The customer would place the order and SAP would spit out an estimated 90-day scheduled delivery date. It would often take a whole week to get to a "reasonable" delivery date.

When we conducted our gemba walk we asked, "Why are we quoting 7-21 days to the customer?" It turned out that the numbers in the system were arbitrary. Product management placed the lower number as an 'aspiration' date. There was nothing statistical or fact-based about this date. Product management then cut and pasted this date for all products that had a similar product structure. This cutting and pasting of an aspiration date was problematic. Why? Because even though products had similar bill of material (BOM) structures, 70% of the components were totally custom to ADC. Worse yet, we often sourced these components to a single small mom-and-pop supplier. These small suppliers did not stock any of these custom components, so when we received an actual customer order our suppliers quoted us their longest lead-time, often 60 to 90 days.

Then where did the "21 days" of the "7 to 21-day" lead times come from? Our master schedulers semi-arbitrarily picked a date that they "thought" they could hit. However, this range was not based on any statistics whatsoever. If we did not have finished goods stock on the shelf, there was little to no chance we could manufacture the products in 7-21 days. In essence we were giving false expectations to our customers.

And this was just the beginning of the gemba walk! From quoting, we would walk through the process of order entry. What steps did we take to enter the order in the system? Would you believe that we entered and re-entered the order in multiple systems multiple times? This is common in many companies.

Once the order was in the system a material planner would start looking at components and capacity based on what order was "hottest." Since we were expediting in an uncontrolled fashion the material planners would schedule and reschedule production runs multiple times during the day. I don't think I need to tell you that changing a production schedule multiple times in one-day results in massive inefficiencies.

Finally, the planner would release the order to the factory floor and the manufacturing line supervisor would attempt to finish the order before the due date.

For this gemba walk, we had to talk to dozens of people across multiple facilities to get an accurate picture of what they actually did. In the factory we physically walked wherever the materials went. We discovered some very interesting findings:

We filled a semi trailer with sheet metal parts to travel a distance of 100 feet to go from one building to another. This added an extra day of queuing time.

At the end of each day workers used bubble wrap and packaged the product at every stage of building. There was back-and-forth movement in and out of our warehouse with SAP transactions to track every movement of the subassemblies. This added days and days, if not a week of extra queuing time.

The entire process of kitting (gathering components from the warehouse for a production order) took 1-3 days to go from the warehouse to the factory floor. If you followed the process throughout the factory, through different process steps, in and out of the warehouse, you would end up walking several miles.

Without a gemba walk, we would never have uncovered all of these transactional and process wastes. No wonder it often took us 40 – 50 days to get orders out the door to customers!

What's the key to a gemba walk? Walk the ENTIRE process. Leave no steps out. Ask lots of questions of everyone who is touching the process. Ask dumb questions (in a polite manner) like "Why do you do that step?" or, "Do you know why you are doing this?" You will often find that people are just following instructions even though they know that what they are doing is inefficient.

Map it visually

Once you walk the entire process, capture that process visually. Lean Sigma methodology has different tools called "value stream maps" or "swim lane diagrams." These are just representations of a process on one sheet of paper.

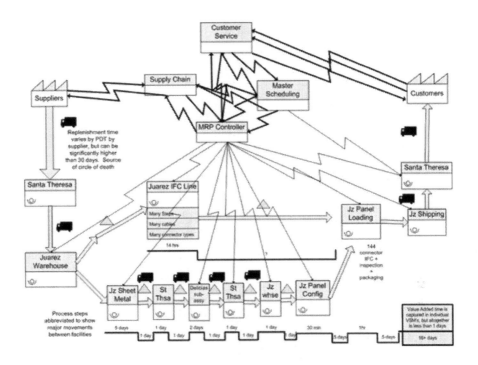

In a value-stream map there are two "flows:" the information flow and the material flow. People often hone in on the material flows, that is, how a product gets built. What often gets neglected or given short shrift is the information flow.

For example, in many companies each process step (sheet metal, painting, molding, assembly) is controlled by a different material planner. Even if a process flows from one process step to another, each process step material planner provides different schedules to the overall master scheduler. Here's what happens in real-life: every material planner "hedges" and "pads" his/her schedule. So, although the amount of time required between one process and the next is only one day, the planners add one week to their schedule. By the time this all rolls up to the master scheduler, the final product has a lead-time of 40 days when it should only take 3 days to physically make the product.

It's hard to know or quantify that this is happening until you walk the gemba and then draw the process on one sheet of paper. People operating in their little silos have no idea the impact their actions have on the overall process. In a kaizen event, all the people who touch a process finally see the big picture end-to-end. Just seeing the process as it really exists is powerful. Rather than beat people up to improve, the improvements jump out at them as they study the process map.

Identify waste

Have you ever met someone who collects things? He or she may have stacks and stacks of newspaper or magazines or any number of items. Are they aware of their clutter? Nine times out of ten they don't even realize the clutter exists. That is the way it is with what Lean Sigma practitioners define as "waste." People who live with waste, do things in a wasteful manner day after day oblivious to it. No one does these wasteful activities in a vile and mean spirited manner. They are just following instructions.

In Lean philosophy, value is anything that transforms the form, fit, or function of a raw material to conform to a customer's specifications. Secondly, value means that the action performed must be done correctly the first time. Finally, value means that the transformation is something the customer is willing to pay for. Everything else is waste. Some general rules of thumb are that 80% of activities in a manufacturing setting are wasteful and 50% of activities in a service environment are wasteful.

How do you categorize waste? Lean practitioners use the following acronym: DOWNTIME

> **D – Defects.** A defect is anything that does not conform to a customer specification. In manufacturing this looks like the product not working properly or malfunctioning.

In a service environment this could look like an incorrect bill or shipping the wrong product.

O – Overproduction. In a manufacturing environment what happens is the factory workers receive an order for 1,200 pieces and think to themselves "If I build 2,000 pieces, that will save me from a setup next time." So they build 2,000 pieces and put 800 pieces on the shelf. Let's say the cost to set up a piece of machinery is $150 and the 800 pieces of inventory are worth $2000. The inventory (cash) just sits on the shelf for 12 months gathering dust. Often, after years, it is finally thrown away.

W – Waiting. We all know what this one looks like. Just go to the airport and get in a line. That's waiting. What researchers have discovered is that people hate waiting. They would rather "feel" like they are constantly getting closer to their goal by not starting and stopping. That's why people might drive a few more miles on a highway vs. taking local roads (let's say same travel time) because they hate stopping.

N – Non-utilized Talent. The most lethal form of waste is asking people to shut off their brains and just do what they are told. Keep your mouth shut and keep your head down. You don't have to tell employees this. You just have to shut down their ideas, dismiss their ideas, not follow up on their ideas and pretty soon they stop giving ideas.

T – Transportation. If you see in a manufacturing plant a forklift driving all over the place, that is waste. One, it's dangerous, and two, probably the layout of the plant is wrong. In a service industry, FEDEX and UPS will carefully scrutinize all routes to minimize total driving, left-turns, etc.

I – Inventory. People <u>love</u> inventory. It makes them feel secure. Inventory comes from a "just in case" mentality for contingencies that many times have a very low probability. That's fine except inventory costs money, takes up space, gets damaged, you forget where you placed it and end up buying more of the same thing, etc.,

M – Movement. I had a friend tell me that his plant had their best month ever but people were worried. Why? With their Lean transformation they reduced all excess movement. Things looked and felt calm. Many people feel insecure if they are not rushing around, but in a Lean environment, that is precisely the wrong behavior.

E – Excess Processing. Why do you have to fill out three copies of this or that form? Don't know. Why do you have to keep filling out your name, address, and phone number at the doctor's office? Why do you have to read, print, sign then fax? Why can't I sign the document digitally? These are all examples of excess processing.

It has taken me a very long time to see waste. I could summarize my Lean journey as "learning to see," a phrase borrowed from a book of the same title. The journey to Lean is really about seeing life differently and asking, "Can I do more with less by tapping into creativity and resourcefulness versus wasteful spending?" In America, land of plenty, that mentality is painful. We want more now. That translates into both our personal as well as our professional lives.

Once you see the waste, the team writes it down and shares what they see. They depict the waste they find graphically on a value stream map as targets of opportunity. This forms the basis of corrective actions and countermeasures.

Assign responsibility and follow up

In a weeklong kaizen, if the team can execute as many of the action items as possible on the spot, an incredible feeling of accomplishment is released. This can translate into an overall momentum that will push your project across the finish line.

In a traditional Lean Sigma project the kaizen event is many times considered a "mini-project." For a large initiative like Pull Replenishment, we used these kaizen events as our primary vehicle for pushing this mammoth initiative to the finish line. What you discover is that very little actually gets done in between kaizen events. People are distracted, focused on their day jobs, and unable to coordinate with the necessary players. By bringing people together in one room in an environment of trust and creativity, we constantly broke through roadblocks.

Creating an environment of trust and engagement

It is incredibly difficult to create an environment where people feel empowered. Just getting the right people to the event is a Herculean task, in of itself. Once they are there, they are still thinking about the 100 emails that are sitting in their inbox. People are distracted and a kaizen facilitator must get their brains engaged.

There are several techniques that can assist you. One, establish the ground rules of the event early on. That means people must turn off their cell phones and laptops for the duration of the entire event. Sometimes it is helpful to provide 20-minute breaks or a long lunch where people can break away and get some work done. However, in the meeting room, they must be "all in." We usually penalize people $5 for being late to the meeting, even if it is from a bathroom break. That money goes to a local charity that the team agrees upon. Believe me, I've never seen so many people sprint back to a room to avoid a fee. The technique works but you have to be credible and consistent.

I also like to incorporate several icebreakers and brainteasers to settle people into the kaizen. For personal introductions, we use "two truths and a lie" with great results. People write down three things about themselves on a post-it and hand it in. The facilitator reads them all and the group guesses who the person is and what the lie is. I've learned a lot of very interesting factoids about people. This icebreaker really helps people loosen up. For brainteasers I use word puzzles or "wuzzles." I will flash the word puzzle on a screen and people have to guess a common phrase. We usually make it competitive and assign points for correct answers. Creating a little bit of competition instantly gets people engaged.

So now that people are more focused on the event at hand, I will usually take 30 minutes to give a strategic overview. People want to know where they fit in the cosmic scheme of things, even to the frontline worker. By briefing them, they get a sense of how the kaizen event can "move the ball forward" in a complex initiative.

After those introductory steps, we go through the playbook kaizen event. We conduct a short Lean Six Sigma training module, do a gemba walk, map the process, identify wastes and bottlenecks, and start fixing problems.

If you're in a manufacturing environment it is really, really important to get the plant manager on board with the goals of the event. He or she should physically and verbally endorse the event in front of the group and tell the people that he supports the changes that will be made.

Aside from the plant manager, other key stakeholders must be notified. In a manufacturing environment the maintenance department ends up being a key factor in the success of the kaizen, partly because you end up moving manufacturing lines around and they do the heavy lifting. For other processes, the process owner should either be part of the kaizen or should be at a stakeholder read out. I always brief the process owner well in advance of the kaizen and get her buy-in.

A kaizen event should be about 3 days long for transactional processes and 5 days long for manufacturing processes, as a general rule of thumb. Many times, I will do a mini one-day kaizen event as a follow-up.

Increasing emotional engagement

At the end of each day, I go around to every single person and ask him or her to share one thought or insight they've gleaned. Their comments will range from very profound to humorous. By including everyone, you increase the overall buy-in. People will start to feel like, "This is my project." It will also reinforce key learning. Use this technique liberally and often.

Other key tips for a successful kaizen

RIGHT PEOPLE: Get people who touch the process or the supervisor. If you go up too many layers in the organization, the person attending the kaizen will not know what to change or how. Getting the right people to attend took up the majority of my time. It was a massive pain but was probably the key to overall success.

FOOD: Whenever I host a kaizen, I make sure that the food ordered is really good food. The saying goes that an army moves forward on its stomach. This is true in the business world. I order good food because I want people subtly looking forward to the kaizen event. We always host a team dinner on one of the nights for more team building. My boss does a great job in picking locations with a private room where people can stand and mingle. I love seeing the interactions and socializing that takes place at stand-up dinners.

READOUTS: Keeping the communication feedback loop moving is extremely important. People want to know, "Did we make progress?" Stakeholder readouts both during the event and after the event is complete keep everyone informed and maintain interest and buy-in.

COMMUNICATION BLITZ: Our kaizen master Fab and I produced several videos after different kaizens that we posted on our company intranet. This allowed any interested party to view what we were doing.

The kaizen event ended up being our secret weapon to getting things done. People are so distracted with every day work. We constantly carved our concentrated time every month, sometimes just one full day, and knocked out a huge portion of the work in a live setting. With the right people in the room we got a lot done. Give it a try and see if you don't move the ball forward.

Chapter Eight

Hone in on your strongest levers

In an earlier chapter on "focusing on the critical few" I described how important it was to manage scope. Scope in statistical terms is your "y-variable", or output. Your levers are your inputs or "x-variables". Like the great Archimedes once said, "Give me a lever long enough and I will move the world." For Pull Replenishment, we were able to find two levers that did 90% of the work.

After we finished the first project my boss asked me how long it would take to get 80% of the Americas revenue on Pull. Not knowing much (a fact that has changed little), I said, "Two years." I then mapped out a very elaborate project plan going product line by product line through a Lean transformation.

When I say "Lean transformation," I mean what many Lean practitioners typically imagine: Lean U-shaped cells, one-piece flow, visual management, kanban bin replenishment, supermarkets and the like. (Don't worry about understanding all of those terms; there is no quiz at the end.) In other words, I made an exhaustive plan that included pushing every lever possible within the manufacturing process.

Not wanting to see me flail about haphazardly, our director of Supply Chain, Randy sat me down. Taking interest in my cause he sat me down and helped me find my first lever. "You know David, I think you're doing a great job," he started off, sincerely. "You brought people together from across all functions, which is a very hard thing to do. I'd like you to *consider* what I have to offer. Take it for what it's worth. Think it over and let me know what you think." Randy has such a nice way with words. (I called him "one of the three wise men: Bill, Shiv, Randy.") Not only did he possess great knowledge but also his mentoring style was so pleasant.

"Here's my thought," he continued. "I bet you can get to that 80% of revenue goal in one year, simply by enabling the supply chain. Making our manufacturing process Lean is important, but let's think about *decoupling* that from what we're doing with the supply chain. If I focus my guys on enabling 80% of the volume of our components that support Pull Replenishment, I'll bet we get most of the way there by focusing on that lever. In fact, I'll put all of my commodity managers supporting this instead of chasing cost savings. Think about it," he said, and left me alone to ponder.

What's great about creating momentum is that once you demonstrate a winning, viable strategy, sometimes key people show up wanting to help you. In this case, Randy showed up big time. He took all of his commodity managers like a stack of cards and handed me three aces. After consulting with the other wise men, Bill and Shiv, I agreed with Randy's decoupling strategy. The great thing about leading a movement is that I don't have to come up with the great ideas. I just have to give great ideas enough runways to take off, and in this case, this idea ended up being crucial.

We decided to decouple Lean manufacturing from supply chain enablement. Our Black Belts and Master Black Belts would continue transforming our manufacturing lines, but at a different cadence and timeline.

Our team validated and further strengthened the second lever from the original project, that being our "no expedite" policy. My original hypothesis around transactional waste and operational disruption came from my experience driving to work every day on the I-405 in Southern California from Torrance to Irvine. This unpleasant ritual taught me about everything from the origins of road rage, post-modern isolation, why the U.S. is a driving culture, to understanding the theory of constraints.

I used to carpool with my friend Biz in the HOV (high occupancy vehicle) lane. As we passed by thousands of cars moving at a snail's pace Biz would grin, look over and say "Later dudes" or sometimes just "Laters!" We often would whiz past miles and miles of traffic at a standstill. "Biz, do you think there's an accident somewhere up there?" I would ask. Several miles up the road what we usually saw was this: cars merging from an on ramp driving slower than 70 mph would cause drivers to hit their breaks causing a ripple effect backwards. This ripple effect looked like a slinky of cars accelerating and breaking, worsening further back from the initial cause until all cars were at a standstill.

This slinky effect mirrored what we saw when we dealt with sales order expedites. While at customer service it appeared that we could manipulate order schedules, further back in the supply chain our suppliers were more locked into their schedules. We actually created more problems than we solved using expedites.

How did expedites create problems? In essence they stole capacity and materials from other orders waiting in line. Once the capacity and materials were used by expedites we would often discover, "Oh, no! We have no more components. Our supplier for this part gives us 60-day lead times." This would cause several orders to come in at 100+ day lead times. The more we pulled things in, the more other orders would slingshot out in terms of delivery schedule.

To solve this we decide to shut off expedites as much as possible. This was the manufacturing equivalent of creating an HOV lane with traffic dividers separating Pull from non-Pull. We wanted Pull parts to go as fast as possible in their HOV lane without operational disruption. Amazingly, just focusing on those two levers enabled us to get to 14-day lead times with a 95% service level.

This honing in on the strongest levers is the opposite of what management consultancies propose. In all of the projects I've seen where a consultant was involved, the consultants proposed solutions that were elegant yet too thorough for their own good. One reason might be that these consultants are trained to think about solutions that are "mutually exclusive, collectively exhaustive (MECE)." Such thinking is fine in terms of thinking out-of-the-box. Such thinking is expansive and often times fresh. However, MECE does not take into account the organization's ability to execute such expansive plans. We honed in on our strongest levers, and got the "biggest bang for our buck."

Chapter Nine

Recognize Every Day Heroes

One of the more counterintuitive approaches we took was to increase the amount of recognition we gave to employees. A more initial instinct would have been to create a burning platform, show how broke the current system is, show a future state, and then show everyone how short they fall from that future state. Presumably, by shaming people, they will endeavor to take the mark of shame off their back and will perform.

I have heard that this approach works for CEO-types like Steve Jobs. His standards of perfection are so high that he keeps his employees feeling inadequate, like they're never living up to his expectations. Some companies essentially thrive off a model of, "Hire, train, retain, and move up or out insecure overachievers." This approach works in certain cases, but like I said, we chose a different route, more in line with our culture.

Quickly recognizing positive behaviors

In order to create dramatic change, I chose to focus on everything employees were doing right, were doing well, and worth noting. At every opportunity I told stories about actions key people took and then proceeded to hand that person a five-dollar Starbucks card. It was a glorified pat on the back, but we found that this initiative ran on caffeine, literally.

It happened during the very first kaizen. One of the key tenets of kaizen events is to bring the *right people* to the table. At the time, I did not know who all those *right people* were. A guy from IT named Bob realized that a couple key people were missing. I did not know either of the gentlemen so I asked Bob to invite them to drop everything they were doing to participate in this week long kaizen. Bob called them, communicated with their superiors, and within a couple hours both were participating in the kaizen. They ended up being two very important project members.

So, the next morning as we started the next full day of kaizen activities, I paused and retold this story to the whole team. We called Bob up front and gave him his Starbucks card. Everyone applauded. I said, "Listen, anytime someone does something worth noting, tell me."

Amazingly, public recognition had a truly synergistic effect. People conducted themselves in ways big and small that had a massive cumulative impact. And I'm referring to tangible shareholder value. We spent easily over $10M on consultants, software, and new hires over the previous four years with little discernible results. For Pull Replenishment's first year, we spent zero dollars in CAPEX, hired no additional full-time employees, and used no consultants. People's productive output increased and covered all the gaps of what normally we would have budgeted millions of dollars for.

Overwhelming bad behaviors by focusing on the good

Making people feel good about their positive contributions snowballed. I wrote previously that we used the kaizen event as one of the main vehicles for empowering employees to make changes. Once they were empowered, encouraged, and recognized for doing right things, the project just took off. I could not keep track of everything people who were formally part of the Pull Replenishment team and those who were seconded by others were doing to move the initiative forward.

I would sit in on Green Belt training and lo, and behold, there were prospective Green Belts briefing about their projects that were designed to help Pull Replenishment. I would receive Power Point presentations of completed projects that were moving Pull Replenishment forward.

It was during those moments that I realized we had, indeed, created a movement. People were executing Pull Replenishment independently, decentralized, with a lot of initiative.

After we finished a completed "wave" of projects, we held a ceremony to recognize all who participated and contributed. I took a page from the Master's Tournament – I thought the green jacket ceremony at the end was so cool, so we did our own version. We did the white lab coat ceremony, with a custom crest and name embroidered on the front. In Juarez, Mexico, they wear these smocks and lab coats as part of their job. We included all front line employees who participated in Pull Replenishment and gave hundreds of lab coats to them. The lab coat became our symbol of transformation.

My favorite question over the months came from people who would stop me and ask, "How do I get my lab coat?" That was how I knew transformation was happening. The initiative itself became a "pull system." We didn't recruit people. They asked to join.

It makes sense, doesn't it? Much of the time people toil for a manager who neither recognizes their hard work nor their accomplishments. They feel under-appreciated. We decided in the free market of ideas, people were going to gravitate to working on something where they got recognized, where there was visible momentum, where they would feel good about themselves. It worked. Within ten months we went from about twenty people to several hundred people working on Pull Replenishment. No one reported directly to me. But somehow, they knew the vision that Bill laid out and actively worked to accomplish it.

Our people stared at the challenge in front of them and met the challenge head on. I think about the thousands of man-hours that were required for us to be successful and how everyone worked tirelessly without complaining. Honestly, they made my job easy. Sometimes I'm ashamed at how little I actually did.

I encourage you to take five extra minutes to say 'thank you' to people. Sure, they're just doing their job, but if you want results that surpass "just doing their job description," sincerely thank them. This is as powerful as giving large financial incentives with none of the negative consequences.

Less metrics, more leadership

I admit that many times I focus on people's weaknesses, errors, and mess-ups. It's easy to see, isn't it? We are adept at seeing the speck in our brother's eye. In my earlier years, I felt a strong need to "hold people accountable." Create metrics, formulate plans and timelines and then hold people's feet to the fire. While some elements of creating and maintaining accountability work well, we sometimes miss the fact that behind metrics and accountability are people who need to be motivated.

The next area where I fell short regarding human motivation was a mechanistic view of performance management. I felt strongly that everyone needed to have the same goals in their performance plans with incentive plans toward those same goals. In previous initiatives we did have many, many people linked toward common goals through the official performance management system with clearly designed incentives. We even had a special bonus plan designated for meeting certain goals.

All of these measures work on paper, but in our case, even with the presence of formal incentive plans and goal alignment, people did not find the motivation to carry through on their projects. Perversely, the special incentive plan created resentment both from without the group and within, and in some cases, had the opposite of the intended effect. Within the ADC culture, some people did not want to be singled out as being part of this special incentive program. Or, for those who had to work on the project but were not included on the special incentive program, they felt resentment and did not want the initiative to succeed.

In contrast, our success in Pull Replenishment revealed motivation can be encouraged with just a few simple things: 1) Give people autonomy to do meaningful work. 2) Give small, but frequent public and private recognitions 3) Give specific, behaviorally based praise.

In the first case, many times the top-down, metrics driven, incentive driven approach carried a heavy burden for the people executing the plan. We would spend lots of time arguing about metrics. Were the metrics the right metrics? What was the baseline? What was a reasonable goal? What was a reasonable stretch target? Who was to keep score? This grueling process drained the organization and wasted time.

In Pull Replenishment, I never checked to make sure that everyone was aligned from a performance management standpoint. Ironically, I did not care if team members officially had the same goals that I did. Instead, I tried to create a work environment where people felt good about participating in the project. They could use their creativity, their skills, and their talent and get intrinsic reward from seeing the project executed successfully. Did Shiv or I stand over people's shoulders to monitor their work? No. We trusted that people were doing things the right way, even if on occasion their approach was less than optimal, or not an approach we would have used ourselves.

Setting your people free

By allowing people to work freely, they could feel pride in their unique contribution to the team. Whatever they did was not the result of some robot-like response to an overly orchestrated project plan. Shiv and I managed things fluidly, allowed people to make mistakes, but overall, focused on when people did things right.

This brings up the second case; we learned to give frequent public and private recognition. This is the fun part of human motivation. Not everyone responds to recognition the same way. Some people long for public recognition. Other people want a quiet, person-to-person approach. I have yet to find someone who truly wants zero recognition. Maybe those people exist, but I have not met anyone who does not stand a little taller, try a little harder, and give a little more when he/she gets a pat on the back with a genuine "well-done." I mostly used $5 Starbucks cards as my default way of saying "good job." The majority of people I know drink coffee. And a $5 card is small enough that no one got jealous of another person for receiving one. In fact, I erred on the side of giving these out too liberally. Who cares if I gave out one too many $5 gift cards? What did I have to lose? But the emotional gain created by giving one was many times the value of a silly little card. People just want to feel good about what they are doing. Nine out of ten people are really giving their best every day. They are already getting paid for that work, but it never hurts to recognize a good deed.

So, the third point that is related to giving frequent recognition is to focus on specific behaviors. People feel awkward at receiving praise and recognition when they don't know why.

They might feel unworthy or feel like the praise is disingenuous. My approach was to write down on a little card the actual specific action or behavior I was recognizing. I would try to send a card as close in time-proximity to the observation as possible in order to reinforce the behavior. Or, at a meeting, I would tell a quick story to the whole team about someone's specific behavior that I appreciated. "Hey team, I just wanted to point out what Lori has been doing. She has proactively communicated her progress on her deliverable and has used active listening to make sure she understands where other people stand." You could say that most of my job was to act like a glorified cheerleader.

At the start of the project, I was a little concerned that I did not possess the formal levers of aligning people's incentives and metrics in place, but what I discovered was something more valuable. Money is not the only thing that motivates people. We like to say that our initiative ran on "recognition and caffeine."

Customize your recognitions

Although I liberally gave out Starbucks cards, I also tried to find little recognition items that uniquely fit the personalities of our core team. For example, one of our team members didn't drink coffee but liked lemon candy, so that's what I bought her. Because I knew my good friend Shiv ate a lot of ketchup with his food, I bought him a big bottle of Heinz ketchup and affixed a custom sticker I made with his face on it. I did the same thing for Fab but with a can of Illy Espresso. For my boss Bill, I had a plaque made with a bow tie as the centerpiece commemorating our success. Why a bow tie? Because Bill wore one every week and the bow tie became a signature item for him. He loved it. For a couple of ladies who did love coffee, I ordered customized Starbucks cards with cartoons of them on the card saying "First Pull Replenishment, next the world!"

You might not memorize every factoid about your team but knowing that Melissa drinks a venti skinny cinnamon dolce latte is one way of communicating that you care about the details of her life.

Chapter Ten

Focus on the Right Metrics

The longer I'm in corporate America, the more I am convinced that what are generally accepted as key performance indicators (KPIs) conceal and distort reality more than give an accurate view of the business. They are meant to be a management tool to understand what drives the business, displayed beautifully on dashboards and scorecards. Instead, KPI's cleverly astound and confuse the bewildered spectator with a smoke and light show. Conquering the bewildering world of KPI's is an immense, backbreaking task, but it is an absolute pre-requisite for creating transformation.

Here's how KPI's work: it should be fairly easy to calculate revenue (though after Enron, even reporting revenue is highly suspect). It should be fairly easy to calculate gross margins and management income. What gets more difficult is to peel back the layers behind revenue and margins to understand what drives the business, hence the un-fancy term "business drivers." If you understand the business, these drivers should be intuitive. Business drivers include *on-time delivery, customer satisfaction, cycle-time, manufacturing yield*, and other productivity metrics. Each of these drivers breaks down into sub-metrics. Ideally, people on an operating level should be able to understand the sub-metrics, and act in a manner corresponding to improving both the metric, and ultimately, profitability.

Unfortunately, many of these metrics are developed in functional isolation. When aggregated at the company level we find that different groups are working at cross-purposes with one another. But by God they are driving their KPIs! For example, a favorite metric within manufacturing environments is something called "earned hours." If you own a lot of machinery, essentially you want to drive a high percent utilization. Within a build-to-forecast environment, the outcome is often unfortunately a lot of inventory that the company ends up throwing away.

Say customer demand for a certain widget is 100 pieces. The machine operator says to himself, "I don't want to set up the machine again so I'll build 400 pieces and put the other 300 on the shelf. That way when the customer orders in the future we can immediately ship their order."

Again, this ended up having disastrous unintended consequences for ADC. There was no coherent stocking strategy, so a customer would randomly receive shipments next day for low runners (SKU's with low annual revenue) but ironically have to wait 40 days for a high runner. When we studied lead-time performance by part number, we found that there was no rhyme or reason to what a customer would experience.

Whenever the Lean Sigma team would try to alter this KPI of earned hours, we met with fierce resistance. After operating for 30 years under this earned hours paradigm, many simply could not believe what the data showed.

Another KPI that can have a disastrous unintended consequence is paying salespeople purely on revenue (Revenue per Salesperson). In a portfolio environment where the margin profiles by products could vary 40% - 50%, we could generate high revenue dollars but perform miserably on operating profit. We had a particularly nasty product line that generated something close to -30% gross margins. When management decided to kill the product line, Sales and Product Management erupted in a turf war. Sales couldn't understand how we could be so customer unfriendly by not offering the customer a product they wanted. Earning this piece of business was a huge win for the lead sales person (high Revenue per Salesperson) but a massive loss for the business. This was yet another example of how following KPI's pitted functions against each other.

So where do we see the smoke and light show? Camp out at a monthly executive business review and you'll start to see the magic. Here's how the magic typically works. About two weeks before a monthly meeting someone will send out a notice to the different KPI owners. Many companies use some sort of green, yellow, red designator with the KPI. Obviously if your KPI measurement is "green," you're good to go, no questions asked. If you report "red," then you'll get assigned "help." This is the business version of staying after school for remedial training.

The funny thing you will notice is how few KPI's will ever report a red status. The KPI owners will massage the metric, or explain special circumstances that should not be included in the official metric. Their report will sound something like this: "My KPI 'all-in' is at 75% but 'adjusted' is at 85% when we factor out the tornado we experienced in Kansas and the flood we experienced in Tennessee. {another 5 minutes of narration} So my KPI is green for the month." Usually by taking management on the scenic route of the business, most business leaders give the briefer a pass.

Creating useful metrics, a monstrous task

In my case, we had to measure on-time delivery. When I started my project we had multiple metrics for on-time performance. There were *ship-to-request, ship-to-target,* and *ship-to-promise.* We tracked each of these and reported on them in monthly meetings. Oh, and when there was a negative trend, we moved heaven and earth to right the ship. Unfortunately, for us that meant overbuilding inventory.

You would think that something simple like *"ship-to-request"* would accurately reflect our performance vs. customer expectations.

(*Ship-to-request* is the percent of orders that were shipped to customers by the date they requested.) But, here's the rub. What happens when 80% of our orders have a request date of zero days? If you are a distributor or a retailer then you can measure how many times you ship from inventory without a stock out. However, if you are a manufacturer like ADC, it becomes physically impossible to create enough inventory to satisfy customer request dates of "today" and run a profitable business. Over the years our customers learned that we would jump through hoops to hit their request dates. When we offered a limited set of products, we somehow made the business model work. As the number of SKU's we offered exploded in proliferation, we simply could not ship products to meet customer request dates. Thus, we created the "circle of death" to figure out which zero-day request date order we would work on. Customers and salespeople learned over the years to game the system. People started putting in "Jan 1, 1900" as a request date. Why? Because the order would show up as past due by about 10,000 days and hopefully get worked on before the others. The only time we would hit our "zero days" request would be when we happened to have inventory on the shelf. Since we offered over 80,000 SKUs to the market, we would only guess correctly 40% of the time. So *ship-to-request* essentially became a worthless metric because so many orders had false request dates.

On the other side of the spectrum we had *ship-to-promise*. Even though we might have quoted "7-21 days" for a lead-time, when the purchase order was placed it would immediately be confirmed at "99 days." A customer service agent would have to expedite just to get a semi-reasonable lead-time. After the expedite, operations and supply chain would have 48 hours to respond with a better lead-time. So "99 days" would turn into "60 days." The customer or sales person would "escalate" the order and "60 days" would turn into "50 days." Once again, the customer or sales person would escalate, and "50 days" would turn into "40 days, last and final." After exhausting everyone, that 40-day commitment or "promise" would get locked in the system and voila, we would deliver 97% ship-to-promise. Every month at our management meetings we would report our 97% ship-to-promise metric and say to ourselves, "See, we are meeting our commitments to our customers!" Never mind the fact that the product that we shipped in 40 days was originally quoted to the customer at 7-21 days.

John, our favorite Sales VP, scratched his head and said, "This is ridiculous. I ain't the smartest person on the planet but this 97% does NOT reflect customer satisfaction." So, he stormed into my boss' office to change things. Like Jesus in the temple, you could say he overturned the tables.

What was absolutely maddening about the situation was that it took me probably 90 days just to understand how we calculate on-time delivery and what we meant by all the different metrics. You see, no one knew. Talking to different people across different functions, everyone had a different operational definition of what a "lead time" was. What? We don't know what "lead time" means?

What compounded the confusion was the fact that we created a process called "sales alerts." This was something like a "maybe" order. It was invented by sales to get ahead of the game. Even though only 50% converted into an order we treated sales alerts like real orders and began production. So, when *did* the clock begin? If a sales alert converted, the sales department would complain "I gave you the sales alert 100 days ago and you still don't have the order done yet?"

We decided the only way to get out of this bottomless pit was to make our operational definitions simple and clear. "*Lead time* is the number of days from when the order books to when the order ships out of our distribution center. We measure ourselves against calendar days, not business days." Then we asked Sales, "What would be a good, aggressive lead time that would help you win the business?" They replied, "How about 14 days?" "O.K.," we replied. When Operations and Supply Chain heard this, you could see their collective jaws drop. Their planning time default of 90 days was their way of protecting themselves from these outrageous Jan 1, 1900 requests.

Something had to give. The circle of death had to stop. "We're going to commit to 14 days so that Sales will agree to stop expediting," I said. The team agreed. With that, we decided to judge ourselves against an objective metric, *ship-to-target*. We would align the systems so that the quote, the planning time fence, and the target lead times would all align around 14 days. We would judge ourselves against a 95% standard.

Just by cleaning up operational definitions and metrics we could align the entire company from Sales through Supply Chain around a common goal. I know this sounds elementary, but just getting to this point took a whole lot of internal selling. When we started executing against a 14-day target lead-time, everyone operated under a common set of assumptions and a common script. We would quote 14-days and get the order. No more "maybe" sales alerts would generate production orders. Sales now knew the rules-of-engagement. Close the deal, get the order, and we'll commit to 14 days. It worked like a charm. We immediately were able to ship to our 14-day target with a 95% service level once we initiated Pull.

Getting on the same sheet of music

The first lesson I learned was to question all assumptions implicit in a metric. Why are we measuring things the way we do? What does this metric really mean? How do you calculate it? How do ordinary people from frontline sales, to frontline customer service, to front line manufacturing operators understand this metric? What I have found is that more times than not, a few people do understand the metrics, but they have difficulty communicating the metrics to the masses.

Imagine an orchestra with each player looking at sheet music. The title on the score is "Beethoven's Ninth Symphony." But one set of music is set at 4:4 time, another at 3:2 time. Or one score is in the key of D, the other is in the key of F#. You already know how the music will sound – horribly. And yet this is exactly how many companies operate. How in the world do they make money?

You can criticize how we defined "lead time." You can tell me "lead time should go from order-receipt to when the customer receives the shipment, not when you ship from distribution." Indeed, different companies have different operational definitions. Right, wrong, or indifferent, we picked a definition and stuck to it. And by making it simple, clear, and easy to understand, we dramatically improved our ability to serve customers.

Chapter Eleven

Build Bridges and Walk Across

My Comfy Silo

One thing that was obvious during four years of failed initiatives was that our company worked in silos. It was very difficult to get the different functions to talk to each other, let alone work together. The functions worked on different goals to the point where functions worked against each other. Building bridges and working toward a unified vision became one of the most difficult tasks, but once accomplished, yielded the biggest dividends.

It worked like this: Product Management, representing the business unit (what we called the "BU"), would develop all new strategies and initiatives. At ADC, Product Management was like the hub of a wheel. All other functions interfaced with Product Management. They were the seat of power and many top executives came from Product Management.

In our company, however, Sales did not report to a general manager. The global sales organization was rolled up into its own structure where the Global VP of Sales reported directly to the CEO. (I could write even more chapters about the consequences of this organizational structure, but since my book is intended to be positive, we'll skip those details). So, Product Management would spend months devising all sorts of strategies and would lead all sorts of initiatives and then spend the next six months fighting with and trying to convince the sales organization to align themselves with the business unit's strategies. It was like the BU would bake a cake, present it to Sales, and upon tasting it, Sales would puke all over it. Unfortunately, since Sales did not report to the BU, nothing got resolved. Many times leaders in the BU tried to swing organizational influence by changing Sales' compensation plans or performance goals, all with little effect. In hindsight, the sales organization was actually the seat of power in the company and everyone knew it. They never lost an internal fight and had the greatest veto power, the threat of losing revenue. "If we do what you say, we'll lose ALL our customers. We have to change course." Since no one in the senior executive team had a sales background, the bluff always worked.

Into this complicated organizational reality, I had to wade and figure out how to align Sales, Customer Service, Product Management, Operations, Supply Chain, and IT. I went through my options: "Let's see, Option 1 is let the BU work on their plans in isolation and then present the plan to Sales. Number of times I've seen this successful? *Zero*. Option 2 is to work with Sales from day one, get their buy-in and see what happens. Hmm…probability of success is at least higher than zero. Let's go with Option 2."

Speaking across silos

I decided to reframe the entire initiative around *sales enablement*. My pitch to the sales team was this: "You're right, delivery sucks and we've set you up for failure. If I were in Sales, I would be ticked off as well. Would you be willing to work with us?" I tried this pitch with a couple of sales executives that I had personally developed a relationship with. One incredibly open and forward-looking executive named Joel decided to play ball. "O.K., I'll help." He sent his direct report to work on the team.

Having Sales representation from day one ended up being a decisive factor in the success of the initiative.

We did not ask too much from Sales in terms of time commitment. Since they were focused on retiring their quota, all I asked was that they constantly be involved as a sounding board.

Were we on the right track? Are we acting in our customers' best interests? How do we properly message this with our customers?

As Shiv and I reviewed the data, one thing became clear. All the expediting we were doing did nothing to actually improve overall lead times. It was like an optical illusion. Every once in a while an expedite would escalate up to a sales vice-president. The sales VP would make several angry phone calls and the whole organization would move heaven and earth to pull in an order date. We would air freight components, work overtime and micro-manage an order till it shipped. On occasion, all of this activity would result in a faster date. What people did not see was the number of orders that got dropped in the process.

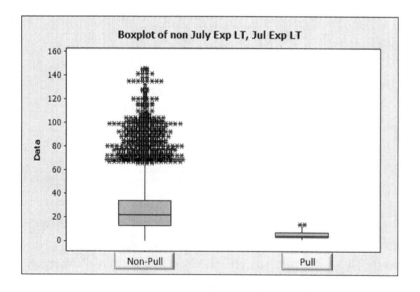

If you understand statistics, the picture above might make sense to you. The data marked "Non-Pull" represents lead times from orders that booked and shipped using our usual expedite method. The "Christmas Tree" effect is the number of outliers past the usual 4th quartile of data. Those hash marks represented *thousands of times*

we dropped the ball even as we pulled in lead time dates on other orders. We called this the bullwhip-effect.

Even if the graphic is difficult to understand from a statistical point-of-view, I think you can see that we did not have control over our processes.

Shiv and I understood the implications of the data. Simply, we had to create a process where we dramatically cut the number of times we were expediting to remove the bullwhip-effect. Since Sales instinctively pushed the "expedite button" to move in dates, we braced ourselves for a massive internal fight over our recommendation. I scheduled an all-day meeting with several sales executives to go over the data.

After we walked through all the data and our plans to improve lead times, one sales VP named Jeff said, "You don't understand. We don't want to expedite. But it takes us a week just to get a lead-time locked in. And the lead times we get are bogus. We have to expedite just to get the organization to commit to a semi-reasonable lead-time. If you're telling us that you'll commit to a 14-day lead-time in 24 hours, we'll gladly stop expediting. We'd rather spend the time with our customers!" Problem solved.

It was amazing. This was just one of many times we found that we were operating under false assumptions. Why? Because people in silos did not talk to each other and validate their assumptions. In this case, Sales told us they wanted to spend time closing deals, not chasing orders. We were solving the root problem and thus taking away the need to expedite. Rather than blind-side them with the upcoming changes, they worked with us every step of the way and validated our decision making process.

As we continued to roll out our initiative, the sales team acted as our biggest cheerleader. And why wouldn't they be? By improving the 95% service level of lead times from 50 days to 14 days, they looked better in the eyes of the customer. They would lose face less and stop apologizing for shipment delays. They would book and ship faster, thus retiring their quota faster. This was indeed a *sales enablement* initiative.

Extra, Extra! No one cares about Productivity Initiatives

By repositioning the initiative as a sales enablement project, we capitalized on the natural bent of our organizational culture. Looking back at previous failures we noticed that the organization quickly grew tired of and lost steam because the initiatives were too inward facing. Without exaggerating, no one cares about operational efficiency projects. If it happens and we save some money, fine. People just expect it to happen. But anything that required behavior changes in the entire company faced fierce resistance, especially if the project was about operational efficiency. "Can we please talk about customers for once?" one Sales VP would complain.

And he was right. Though these changes were necessary, no one could envision how any of the failed initiatives would enhance the customer experience or generate revenue. Reaching across organizational boundaries meant first recognizing what drove the organization. In our case, we were collectively motivated to please customers, grow revenue, and beat the competition. Framing the initiative in this light made it easy for people in Sales, Customer Service, Product Management, Operations, and Supply Chain to come together.

Reaching across organizational boundaries also means giving people a seat at the table. I was very conscientious about inviting as many people as pragmatic to different meetings and events. If I erred, I tried to err on the side of inviting too many people. What I found in the past was the offended outsider syndrome. "Well, someone obviously forgot to include me in the meeting!" Offended Outsider would then do his best to sabotage whatever meeting he missed.

This took a lot of art to manage as the required players shifted as the initiative grew and expanded. Though I had a core group of about 10 people, there was an additional extended group of about 20 who were important to the initiative's success. How did we handle this? Meeting by meeting, and issue by issue.

The crux of reaching across organizational boundaries occurred during our kaizen events. Because the scope our project was transforming an end-to-end enterprise process, we had to have all stakeholders who touched the process be part of the project. Most Green Belt and Black Belt DMAIC projects, great as they are, are still executed within a silo. The overwhelming reason for this is to manage scope-creep and execute within a reasonable timeframe. Nevertheless, a real *breakthrough strategy* comes as the result of an enterprise-level change.

Lessons Learned

How hard is it to reach across functions? It is incredibly hard. Many people did not know who I was. Why in the world is this random person calling me? I imagined people looked at my emails, meeting invites, and voice mails with a bit of puzzlement. In my particular case, to be fair, I was not totally an unknown quantity. Several times I was chosen to speak at the company's town hall events that were broadcast globally. Nevertheless, it is one thing to possess some name-recognition. It is quite another to ask people to give up whole days or even whole weeks of their time to sit in on meetings or kaizen events. One could say my job was chief salesman for the initiative.

I remember sitting with one manager, begging for resources and presenting the vision. He said to me, "It helps that you are so passionate about the vision. Everything else we do here is just cut and dried." From my time in the Army I knew that people like to be part of something bigger than themselves. Few of us are solely motivated by a paycheck, but who wants to be part of yet another failed corporate initiative? And yet, to succeed, I needed a whole lot of participation across functions. How did we overcome this hesitancy? At the end of the day, team members made their own decision to be part of the movement because compared to their day job, at least they felt appreciated and recognized working on Pull Replenishment.

When I think about how much time I spent cajoling, wooing, asking, begging people across functions to be part of the initiative, what I realize is that if I didn't believe in what we were doing, I wouldn't have spent so much time and energy reaching across boundaries. It is really a pain! People start out really skeptical. Many are silently waiting for you to fail. Who needs the grief? No, I was convinced that everyone I was talking to was absolutely critical to the success of the initiative. One thousand people later (working on Pull), I am even more convinced.

Chapter Twelve

Build Competency into your People

It would be great if empowerment were as simple as pointing to a vision and telling people, "Go for it. Go nuts." Truthfully, some people are as intimidated by a vision as they are inspired by it. I might want to climb Mt. Everest some day, but it's hard to get past the first thoughts of, "How on earth could I do that?" To create a movement with positive, sustainable results, it is important to build competencies.

A competency is a set of tasks that people can perform well unconsciously. In other words, you know when you are competent when you can do something well without trying. In the beginning, we have no muscle memory, and doing new tasks is hard. But with practice, we can master new skills and grow new competencies.

In business, there are many competencies to choose from. Apple's people (and I can't believe it's only Steve Jobs) possess a competency to intuitively understand human ergonomics and human interaction with technology. They make products easy to use, make navigating through features intuitive, and make the overall experience pleasurable. In our case, we chose to grow a Lean Six Sigma competency.

Training means creating evangelists

The usual way companies do competency building is a "butts in seats" approach. For Lean Sigma, the CEO might mandate, "I want 100 new Green Belts, 10 new Black Belts, 200 projects, and 400 kaizen events this year." Because he just created a metric with this pronouncement, the organization spins up and rallies around it.

He appoints a Lean Sigma VP to oversee the program. The Lean Sigma VP hires outside consultants to jump-start and run the training. Hundreds of people sign up for training! Hundreds of people get certified. It's a costly, costly affair. If the CEO has absolute power, like Jack Welch had at GE, with a lot of prodding and aligned incentives, this approach can work. But this book is about starting a movement. What does that look like?

Shiv set out to create evangelists. Fortunately for him, Bill was of the same mind. Both were patient in their approach. Bill gave no number targets to Shiv for training Green Belts. Shiv created a pull system. He broadcast his training to the masses and had several takers. When they emailed him he responded, "Don't show up without a legitimate project that your sponsor wants." Shiv knew that without skin in the game, training was incredibly wasteful.

And it worked. By requiring a legitimate project that a sponsor actually cared about, Shiv weeded through all the people who just wanted to "check the box." Interestingly enough, still only 33% of people who took the class completed their Green Belt project. In other words, if they truly were not motivated enough to both go through two full weeks of training as well as complete a project, then Lean Sigma wasn't important to them or to their sponsor.

But on the flip side, those who did have the motivation to complete a project became the evangelists Shiv was looking for. They began to infuse the culture with a fact-based, data-driven approach that the company sorely needed. They understood the difference between common cause and special cause. They understood the need to go to the gemba to truly understand a process. They understood how to align a process to takt time. And as these evangelists went back to their day jobs, they slowly but surely improved their corner of ADC.

In the first year of our Lean Sigma deployment we saw substantive improvements across the company. Our factory in Sidney, Nebraska improved gross margins, reduced inventory, and improved human productivity. Our factory in Brno, Czech greatly reduced the amount of floor space required for manufacturing. Our factory in Juarez improved fiber-optic production 50% with no increase in headcount. We had stories we could share and we had passionate evangelists who told the stories. Shiv and I cataloged their stories through videos that we broadcast on our company Intranet.

Sustaining Success

Because we developed an organizational competency, our Lean deployment did not peter out like the many transformations in the past. While there are obvious merits of the "gitter-dun" or "Just do it!" approach to life, the Lean Sigma way eschews action without understanding. Why? Because sometimes action can be a form of tampering, which makes a process worse.

Competency building using Lean Sigma ensures that actions taken follow a rigorous problem solving methodology. Using Six Sigma techniques, we statistically validate the improvements. Finally we standardize the improvements to sustain the improvements. Projects move into the *control phase* of DMAIC to ensure that the discipline required eventually becomes habitual.

I read a Jan 15, 2010 article in the Wall Street Journal entitled "Where Process-Improvement Projects Go Wrong." The gist of the article described the number of times that an organization generates excitement and momentum in undertaking a Six Sigma project. Then, the Black Belt moves on to the next project and everyone's old behaviors return

The control phase of DMAIC is the hardest part of sustaining transformational gains. Why? In short, it's boring. There are no big milestones in sustaining a gain. Management's attention has by then turned to the next crisis or next big thing. The daily discipline doesn't elicit strong feelings.

My personal story with P90X

Several years ago I went to a wedding in Washington D.C.. I stayed at my sister's house and took out the suit I had packed with me. This suit I had not worn in over 5 years, so imagine my surprise when I got dressed and I couldn't button the pants! I had gained two inches in my waist. (Whenever I tell this story I usually turn to my wife and say that it's her fault for feeding me so well.) In order to fit, I had to take my sister's ponytail holder and loop it around the buttons on my pants, creating an extender. I was very embarrassed and self-conscious during the wedding. Suffice it to say, I didn't dance that night for fear the ponytail holder would go flying and I would end up looking like Bill Clinton, trousers down.

When I got back to my sister's place, I turned on the television set and watched an infomercial for P90X. (Now, I'm not much of an impulse shopper but I admit that I did buy an inversion table after watching QVC.) Wanting to shed some pounds, I went and purchased P90X.

Now for the uninitiated, what is P90X? P90X is a home boot camp that is intended to turn soft-bellied people into Captain America. A colleague at work challenged me and we both went through the entire regimen. Bring it! I did hundreds of push-ups, chin-ups, squats...I puked several times, almost passed out a couple other times. I even followed the program and did yoga! So when I finally completed P90X I did what most Americans do in this situation, I purchased the P90X t-shirt.

The next morning I turned on the television set and popped in my P90X DVD and then turned off the television and ejected the DVD. *"This P90X sucks! I am never going to do this again."* Would you believe that two years later my waistline looks exactly the same as when I went to the wedding?

This is how people treat improvement projects in their personal lives and at work. The improvements don't turn into a *competency* until the organization performs the new process habitually. In other words, as in personal fitness, there is no lasting effect from going on a diet or checking the box for a fitness program. The only real change is *life-change*. You have to be convinced that whatever you're undertaking is worth doing and worth doing permanently.

Create new traditions and keep it fun

When a large change initiative completes the improvement phase and moves to the control phase, it is imperative to not only implement the perfunctory tools like "standard work" and "control charts" but to create new traditions that reinforce meaning behind the change.

In our case, I was blessed that our battle captain, Ricardo, had started to create a new tradition out of our daily standup call. The daily standup was something I instituted during the first wave. We used it to monitor daily shipping performance to our target lead times. Over the course of the year we had honed the daily ritual so that within 15 minutes each day all the key players were able to hone in on problem orders and implement countermeasures.

I give all the credit to the core team for sustaining the daily discipline of this standup call. I certainly did not participate in it every day. Ricardo not only ran the call, but infused the call with a sense of meaning that made the ritual something his team looked forward to everyday.

How do you keep these rituals from turning perfunctory? Make it fun. In Ricardo's case he brought a wooden statue he called "Carmen" to the daily call. This ten-inch statue looked like some Polynesian idol wearing a grass skirt. Every day on the call he went through the roll call: "Is Kim here? 'Here.' Check... Cheryl?...'Cheryl's here.' Check... Elias?.... check... Carmen?... 'Carmen's here.' Check." And at the end of the call he would "go round the horn" and ask everyone if they had something to share. "Kim?" Kim would reply "no issues." Ricardo would ask each person until he got to the wooden statue. "Carmen?" Someone would perform his best ventriloquism – "no issues" from Carmen, and then the call would be over. It was a small humorous point during the day, but such things enabled the organization to continue this daily discipline until it became a real competency.

So it is with all competency building. Until new habits are truly formed, it is important to create little hooks that the organization can grab onto that help them see meaning in the ritual.

Chapter Thirteen

Create Culture Change by not Trying to Change the Culture

"You can only move as fast as the culture will allow you to," one wise man once told me. Culture is one of those big, colossal artifacts that will get in your way for creating change. Why? People are comfortable with what they know, and what they know is what they did yesterday. That is usually the same thing they've been doing for the last twenty years. Since there is so much inherent resistance to change in an organization, unless you wield absolute organizational power, it is unwise to fight the culture.

When I was in the mountaineering club at West Point, the instructor said, "If it's you versus the mountain, the mountain always wins." Culture is so pervasive, so strong, so entrenched, that it spits out change agents like an unwelcome foreign object.

Facts + Data does not equal the right answer for your culture

I was hired into ADC as part of VECTOR. There was so much energy and excitement that I felt we were going to change the company. The brightest minds gathered together and split into separate teams to handle different areas: portfolio shaping, order management, design for modularity, etc. When we dug into the data, the facts seemed clear. It seemed we had that burning platform.

For example, I was in the portfolio-shaping group. Upon reviewing the data we found some amazing facts: we had over 80,000 active SKUs, of which only 30,000 sold in any given year. Of those that sold, 15,000 comprised only 1% of revenue. On the other end, only 1,500 SKUs comprised 80% of revenue. This was an incredibly skewed Pareto diagram. The mandate seemed very simple: rationalize the portfolio. Cut the tail!

The culture revolts and begins expelling the change agents

When our team presented the facts to senior management and even the board of directors, they blessed the proposals. Then we went to Product Management and Sales with our findings. You would think facts and data would prevail. Wrong.

"If we don't offer our customers everything, they will go to someone else." "If we don't offer this little widget, customers won't buy the other $1M of products." "We made this company by doing whatever the customer asked." On and on the organization pushed back against the team.

Because senior management blessed the plan, Product Management had to demonstrate compliance. The organization made obsolete 10,000 part numbers that had zero sales in two years. We still created approximately 4,000 new part numbers each year. Essentially, we did nothing to reduce portfolio complexity. Astoundingly, no one shut off the ability to reactivate SKUs, which happened frequently.

The organization showed the results to senior management. Look how many SKUs we cut! Senior management (none of them with an operations background) was thrilled. "Great job team!" Senior management had no insight into the effort required to reduce portfolio complexity. They were satisfied and moved on. The culture effectively stonewalled the initiative. People went through the motions knowing that nothing would result.

Over time, almost everyone hired for the different corporate initiatives left the company. As one person told me,

"There are so many flavors of the month that we just wait until they go away." And go away they did.

Going with the grain of the culture to change the culture

When I received the opportunity to lead Pull Replenishment I had to look in the mirror and ask myself what was going to be different this time? After all, I was one of the few people left who was associated with that initiative that brought me to ADC. If I didn't want to get ejected from the organism like an unwanted foreign object, I had to change my approach. For example, people associated that last initiative with a disdain for what made ADC great. This time around I had to focus on the positive. I meditated on all the reasons why I stayed at ADC. If you don't like the company you're with, people will sense it. It will come out of your pores as you walk around the company despising all the people you believe are resisting change.

There were many things I liked about ADC: the company was full of fundamentally good, honest, hard-working people. They loved to serve the customer and were fanatical about customer service. They loved to win and beat the competition. In my mind, ADC was like *Rocky*, a scrappy underdog who never said die.

I figured if I was going to be successful, I had to focus on and enhance all those qualities I liked about the company. I had to win people over. "Many hands lighten the load," goes one Haitian proverb. One thing was for sure: I couldn't do this alone. I needed help and lots of it.

One of the key sticking points in all of the previous initiatives was that the sales organization believed that implementing the recommended actions would hurt revenue. Instead, I decided to try a judo strategy. We had to make Sales care about the initiative's success. Sales told us that lead time issues

101

were already hurting revenue. Well, Pull Replenishment would become a competitive weapon to gain market share. That theme resonated with sales. 'Time as a weapon'…yes, they liked that.

Looking back at the other failed initiatives, I started to understand. It was like we were showing the organization how we were making sausage. Yuck. Who cares? No one wants to know how sausage is made. They only want to know how it tastes. Pull Replenishment was only a means to an end, which was winning through offering competitive lead times.

No one likes change agents, so don't be one.

No one likes change agents. Many people claim they do, but at the end of the day, the culture of a company reacts violently when change agents actually try to enforce change. In certain companies, it is en vogue for a CEO to hire a lot of ex-military types to implement sweeping changes. It worked at General Electric. Robert Nardelli continued the practice at Home Depot. At Home Depot, was Nardelli able to execute with this veritable army (no pun intended)? Yes. Did the culture change? The literature I've read suggests the culture revolted.

I know. I was hired as a change agent twice. First, after business school I was hired to turn around a small business unit that had been losing money. The script repeats itself: fresh eyes are brought in to enable change. Change agent with fresh eyes starts questioning things. People start feeling threatened. Change agent actually studies data. Data and facts are conclusive: there is a burning platform for change! Culture disagrees. Never mind that most of the time the business is bleeding money. The culture violently reacts; it's not our fault we're losing money! It's the economy…it's the previous boss…it's the customer's fault… Change agent keeps pushing. Culture pushes back. And, as my mountaineering instructor said, "if it's between man and the mountain, the mountain always wins." I failed miserably.

So, when my esteemed boss Bill asked me to lead this initiative, he did not ask me to act as a change agent. He told me to create an insurgency. That is, create a "pull system" of evangelists who will share in the vision, share in the passion, and share in the implementation. Don't carry the burden all alone. Bill's insight was impressive. Instead of embarking on a change agent's suicide mission, how about we try to actually win people over?

WIIFM: your most effective tool for change

I took out my bag of tools from my days as a salesperson. Number one tool, the hairpin universal door opener: WIIFM. "What's In It For Me?" Instead of trying to change the culture, I asked myself, "If I were in Sales' shoes, would I be angry?" Answer: heck yes! (Did sales contribute to the problem? Answer: Yes, but that's beside the point.) Why might someone in Sales be frustrated with delivery? Six Sigma answer: variance. Ordinary person answer: I can't tell what lead-time I'm going to get when I book the order. Non-Lean Sigma trained person's way of coping with the problem: throw a bunch of inventory on the shelf. Six Sigma reason for our lead-time problems: we are always working on the "wrong" inventory in our forecast as the real order books. Too late – the components and capacity are taken by the forecasted finished good.

As we thought through the dilemma from a salesperson's perspective, we came to this conclusion: if I'm in Sales, I don't want to lose face with my customer. So, why don't we set sales up for success by creating a system where we can immediately promise a lead time and deliver to that lead time with a 95% service level? (The reason we chose 95% service level is because achieving a 99%

service level would have been prohibitively expensive to implement.)

In previous initiatives, we never engaged Sales on the front end. This time, we did. We asked them, "if we give you 14-days at a 95% service level, would that be good for customers?" They responded enthusiastically, "We will take market share." And, they added, "Booking and shipping faster means we retire our quota faster and can go on to the next deal." BINGO. We discovered the WIIFM factor. No need to be a change agent. How about making our people successful? Sound better than "you need to change?" Absolutely.

Understanding and empathizing with resistance to change

One reason why we react (and all of us do) so adversely to change is that humans have a notoriously poor ability to guesstimate risk and judge effort. Change always seems colossally difficult, distressingly painful, and full of unanswerable unknowns. As we started our initiative, all the 'what ifs' kept popping up: "What if customers get angry? What if sales people revolt? What if we run out of components and can't hit our 95% commitment? What if our suppliers go bankrupt? What if customers order both 'Pull' and 'non-Pull' parts on the same order?" Probability of occurrence: 100%. Severity of impact: $1B loss.

Because we humans frequently misjudge risk, misjudge probabilities, and misjudge impact, we have the tendency to "freak out" at the start of a change campaign. And that know-it-all change agent just appears too smug. With a few fear-doom-and-uncertainty scenarios that the change agent can't answer, the culture reverts to status quo.

But if you go into a change initiative with a *servant-leader's* heart, that is, "I'm just another guy in the boat with you rowing,"
104

you're able to capitalize on the misery loves company sentiment. "Yeah, yeah, the situation sucks. Yeah, you're right, it's terrible that we trained our customers to behave this way..." Empathizing is key to getting on the same side. What many change agents forget is that "those dummies" are the ones who are going to have to execute the change eventually. Why would they execute for the change agent, to make him look good, when he's trying to prove everyone wrong?

I learned to go with the "I have some extra time that you don't have. You're busy doing important things. How about I work on this thorn in your side?" If you credibly fix problems, people start to trust. At the end of the day, we did not approach Pull Replenishment with a finger in the eye approach. We were genuinely trying to make the customer experience more consistent and the sales people appreciated the effort. Their support made all the difference.

Chapter Fourteen

Empowerment means people will screw up. And that's O.K.

Good management is like conducting an orchestra. You're not playing an instrument and directly producing any sound, but the value you are providing is essential. Most people who become managers are strong individual contributors, much like a first violinist. But a conductor does not simultaneously play an instrument and lead the orchestra. That's precisely what modern corporate managers try to do. Effective managers, like good conductors, lead from the front and trust that each individual can competently perform the task she is given.

With Pull Replenishment, in order to execute on an accelerated time schedule, I had to trust. There were too many variables to manage, too many action items to micromanage, too many people to supervise. So, I delegated deliverables and held weekly follow-up meetings. This is classic project management methodology stuff. So, where does the empowerment and trust really come in?

Let your people own *their* (not *your*) solution

Trust and empowerment come in to play during the brainstorming and solution-selection process. Imagine a typical manager who includes his people in the discussion about different courses of action. They debate and argue. He then swoops in like King Solomon and delivers the approved solution. Since the solution was *his,* he must stand over people's shoulders as they execute and micromanage their actions. "No! The font should be *Cambria*, size

24! The spreadsheet needs to have this column and this row. The dashboard needs to look like this. I'm sorry, but on your slide you put an 'an' instead of 'the.'" Oh, yes, it gets this petty sometimes. I know because I have had executives micromanage my Power Point slides. Other friends have told me their previous managers would micromanage their Excel spreadsheets. Bottom line: this does not engender empowerment.

What I tried was something called the "dumb infantryman" approach. The core team members would generate a solution and present their solution. "Listen, you guys get paid to be smarter than me on these matters. We're going with your solution, but you own it." Other times, team members would occasionally try to weasel out of responsibility by asking for an answer. "Nope, I'm just a dumb infantryman. I don't know the answer. What do you think?" You see, sometimes, if the team knows the answer is a difficult choice, they will let the manager propose the solution so that they can blame the manager for the failure. But, if the answer is always the *team's,* then the team stands or falls together.

How to handle unforeseen setbacks

No matter whether you empower people or not, your project will confront Murphy's Law. Bad things will happen. However, if your people are truly empowered, they will fix the problem themselves instead of throwing up their hands in defeat. A good example of this happened when we calculated our component inventory needs. SAP, our planning software, has a dozen ways to do this and we chose a method called a "Zk-load." The underlying software logic was so technical to me that I said, "Go for it. I trust you guys to choose what you think works best."

So the team implemented this Zk-load process as part of our execution template. On a small scale it worked fine. But when we increased the number of SKUs on Pull to 2500 SKUs, we basically flooded the supply chain with too many orders. The day we loaded the formula in SAP, we created a tsunami effect. We ordered 4x our run-rate of components and caught many of our suppliers flat-footed. Since many purchasers blindly follow SAP, the buyer-planners were releasing orders from the system without understanding the impact. Essentially, the scenario we created was like a python swallowing a pig. We were blindly following SAP and ordering too much inventory.

Now I give a lot of credit to Bill for modeling the correct way to respond to the situation. When I briefed him on what happened he said, "Well, we are learning. This was something we didn't anticipate." That was his way of saying, "O.K., mistakes were made. Just make sure we correct our course of action."

Bill's calm, serene approach to happenstance translated into how I talked with our master scheduler. "Kim, we might have an unintended consequence with how the Zk-load impacts our supply chain." "I know, I know," said Kim. "I'm working with the buyers to release smaller lot sizes so our suppliers don't choke." She had the situation under control. None of us knew this was going to happen. The mistake wasn't fatal, so we just learned our lesson and moved on. No finger pointing, no recriminations, no manager swooping in to save the day. Individuals fluidly took ownership of their actions and continually course-corrected.

Those who own solutions will own and fix the inevitable problems. As a manager, do you really want to own every single problem that arises? You are ultimately responsible, but it sure is comforting when dozens of people are working on solutions even before you are aware that there is a problem.

Good managers allow people the freedom to experiment, implement, course-correct, and ultimately perfect what they are working on. For example, our team in Mexico established a lean

"U-shaped" manufacturing cell. Our Mexico team had to set up and tear down the cell about four times till they got it right. What told me that our initiative was working was that they kept tinkering and trying until they succeeded. In previous initiatives, people would have tried something once, hit a brick wall and then would have thrown their hands up in the air. "See, XYZ change-initiative doesn't work." But with the freedom to experiment and tinker, your team will amaze you with ingenuity and perseverance.

Reduce the gravity of the task at hand

Starting a movement by empowering people is scary, especially if in your mind, so much is at stake. One way of handling things is to create a crisis mentality. "Guys, the Titanic is sinking! We have to move, NOW!" This approach will create a short burst of fear-induced energy. In a true crisis situation, an all hands approach can produce dramatic results. This works well in defusing real world examples like quality recalls, or shipping product to hit month-end revenue.

However, this does not work for fundamentally transforming a company. Transformation requires a long-term, multi-year mindset with constancy of purpose. When a "burning platform" is overemphasized for a transformational initiative, expectations for instant results will run too high. People will burn out quickly.

Remember how important tinkering is? Tinkering does not and should not happen in a crisis. Crises require absolute focus and discipline to a top-down driven mandate. For tinkering to occur, people need to feel safe. If you promote a crisis mentality, people will not feel secure enough to take the kind of risks and ownership required for a large-scale transformation. What they will revert to is doing exactly and only what they are told to do. We call this "CYA."

What does it look like to implement transformation without the "burning platform?" A leader will, above all things, act calmly and not get tripped up with any single monthly result because he knows that what's more important is trajectory and perseverance.

When we rolled out our 3rd Wave of projects, I thought we would get to 70% of revenue on Pull Replenishment. Whoops, I made an error in my calculations. When the numbers came in, we were at around 45%. Some people overreacted. "What the heck? We thought we'd be around 70%. What's going on here?" Not Bill. Even though I made a mistake in my calculation, Bill knew that our forecast was based on modeling a trailing 12-month revenue mix. That's like driving looking at the rearview mirror. Essentially, our product mix changed 50% every year. He knew it was inherently flawed so he didn't come down on me like a ton of bricks when our assumptions came up short.

We often do such a poor job trusting each other, don't we? We can be so scared that other people will mess up that we do all the work ourselves to ensure quality control. But this 'superhero' mode doesn't scale. And people who compensate for their lack of trust become the classic micro-manager.

My focus on empowerment came from a bit of backwards induction. There was no way we would succeed unless everybody was pulling on the oars in the same direction. That meant the team had to own the project. That meant they had to believe in the project. That meant they had to believe in themselves. That meant they had to come up with their own solutions. That meant I had to give everyone the autonomy to do meaningful work and not make them feel badly if things didn't go "my way." That meant I had to manage by clarifying the vision and what it meant for people, but allow people to get the "how" by themselves. In a word, empowerment.

Many hands truly lighten the load and empowering people is the only way in life you, anyone, or I will ever succeed in accomplishing a large-scale transformation.

Chapter Fifteen

"No" is a beautiful word

For some reason many of us hate saying the word "no." It sounds so disagreeable and we all want people to like us, right? So instead of saying "no" we say "yes" to everything, especially if the request is coming from a customer or our boss. What ends up happening is that we grind ourselves and our people to a bloody pulp with less than satisfying results. Bill saved all of us tens of thousands of hours of heartache by saying "No."

"No" means candidly assessing your limitations

The situation started out with some disturbing trends in our shipping metrics, even before the famous sales VP John "come to Jesus" meeting. In monthly management meetings our on-time metrics were slipping. Because we had too many metrics, it was hard even for a veteran like Bill to know what levers to pull (no pun intended) to fix the situation. So, Bill chose the better part of valor and said, "I can't fix delivery on every part number. We have way too many SKU's. This goes against the laws of physics. I can fix 20% of the parts that make up 80% of the revenue, but if you ask me to fix delivery on every part, you might as well fire me."

This was refreshing candor. Before, we would try to solve everything, all at once with disastrous results. Bill had the ability to quickly drive to "no" and then to "But here's what I can do. Will that be sufficient for now?" In confronting Sales, he drove "No, but here's what I can do" to 150 SKUs. It was brilliant on his part and it set me and the whole initiative up for success. I shudder to think what would have happened if Bill had said the typical "Yep, three bags full" and thrown me the problem. I would have failed.

Saying "no" became the underlying way we cut through complexity. Can we add more SKUs? No. Not yet. Can we put the Wireline products on Pull? No. Can we put our Powerworx products on Pull? No. Can we do five different versions of Pull? No. Can we implement Pull globally? No. Not yet. Can we expedite? No. Can we do sales alerts? No. Can we implement new software? No. Can we hire consultants? No. Can we over-key our dates? No. Can we have multiple planning time fences other than 14 days? No.

What we had created before was a death-by-exception system. If everything was an exception to the rule, then there was no rule. If there was no rule, there was no basis for standard work. If there was no standard work, then there were no meaningful metrics. If there were no meaningful metrics, then there was no way to gauge improvement. And that's why we had, as Dr. Shiv liked to say, the equivalent of Brownian motion. This means we had a lot of particle movement but overall the system was stationary.

Say "no" because you're saying "yes" to something better

Because people hate to hear the word "no" we had to come up with a compelling "yes." Our "yes" was Shiv's vision. He called it Pull 2.0, or upon receiving an order, we would manufacture, assemble, and ship it in 3 days. So, we told everyone, "I know that there are many things that are not satisfying with this current version of Pull Systems, but if we hang together our process capability will improve. We will constantly improve our lead times ahead of the competition so that 14 days becomes 10 days, becomes 7 days till we are finally at a 3-day lead-time. If we keep improving our lead times, will we beat the competition?" Everyone replied affirmatively.

Saying "no" to expediting was difficult for our culture. Unlike Amazon.com or FEDEX, we did not price differentiate based on time. So, if we gave a lead-time that the customer did not like, we immediately expedited. This led eventually to a Peter robbing Paul situation where an expedited order took components and capacity from a non-expedited order. Well, no sales person was going to allow this, so everything became an expedite. And when everything is a priority, nothing's a priority.

When we rolled out our 3rd Wave of projects, we increased the number of SKUs on Pull by 10x. That meant 10x the number of times we would say "No." In the beginning, for 36 part numbers this was easy to do. It was under the radar screen and it seemed no one noticed that we weren't expediting. When we turned the rules on for 2,000 part numbers, everyone noticed that we stopped expediting. And half the sales people had paid no attention to our briefings about Pull Replenishment. They felt blindsided.

"What the heck is going on?" they would email. "I didn't know that we couldn't expedite and now my customers are furious with us." We had trained our customer service reps to hold their ground. No expediting unless it was a true emergency. Because we took the time to explain the vision, explain the benefits, and show a roadmap to that greater "Yes," the customer service organization held their ground. For the first time they said "no" to the sales team. Expedites dropped 60% in one month.

By reducing expedites, we took noise out of the system and were able to ship $15M of products, approximately 10,000 line items to a 96% on-time targeted delivery. Saying "no" worked.

Over the years, our culture was shaped on one word: "Yes." Saying "yes" to a customer makes a worker feel good about himself.

When we are able to come through on a "yes" we feel like heroes. Back in the heyday of our growth with copper-based products, saying "yes" was a formula for success.

What we didn't realize is that the "yes" culture developed at a time when we had 60-70% gross margins. If a customer is willing to pay that much money for your products, the only word you can say to her is "Yes." How about I wear velvet gloves and hand-deliver the products to you?

The lesson that people learned over time was not about aligning value-based pricing with customer needs, but that "yes" was the only thing we could say to the customer. Unfortunately, as time progressed, customers consolidated, grew stronger, more demanding, and became downright unreasonable. We sold a product that had -50% gross margins to a large customer because we could not say "No."

Leaders must protect their people and thus say "no"

As a leader, it is our job to protect our people, to give them meaningful work. Meaningful work means giving our people tasks that engage their brains, and require effort and some elbow grease to get accomplished in 40 hours per week. They can work hard and go home knowing that they accomplished much. When we only say "yes" without having a strong, underlying business model, we set them up for failure.

Because we had not matched a process capability with our promises to our customer, we were destined to fail them. So we quoted "7 – 21 days," but did not have the statistical capability to match the quote. Our 95% service level was 50 days. So saying "yes" was in many ways lying.

Saying "no" meant we were promising that we could match delivery with our process capability, and not promising more. With Pull Replenishment we moved the 95% service level in to 14 days, BUT we stressed, we could not promise better until we improved our process capability.

People understood this intuitively, but after 20 years of ingrained behavior, they instinctively tried to expedite and over-drive for better dates. That is why we had to institute saying "No." By stopping expedites we took out the "bullwhip effect" in the value chain and thus were able to maintain our service levels. "No" worked.

Another way to say "no" is "yes, and..."

In a previous chapter, we said that to change the culture we should not try to change the culture. So, implementing a "no expedite" policy seems like a contradiction. A policy of making Customer Service and Sales say "no" in a "yes" culture is not sustainable. If a process change is not *poke-yoke'd*, that is *fool-proofed,* people will find a way to game whatever policy you put in place. What do you do about the instinctive urge to say "yes" to the customer? Don't fight it. Monetize it.

The best way to say "yes" when you need to say "no" is "yes, and...." Instead of saying "no" to a request for a faster date than 14 days, we could implement a tiered value-pricing scheme. In this case, we are very lucky that many, many companies already have pioneered this approach. FEDEX does it. Amazon.com does it. Customers today are used to paying for expedited delivery. You pay a low rate for standard shipping, but for next day shipping, sometimes customers will pay more for the expedited shipping than for the item itself. Customers value speed and convenience.

Expediting is not wrong. Everybody expediting and nobody paying for it is.

You don't have to say "no" bluntly. Simply allow customers to self-select what they value by offering different options of pricing and delivery. "No" still works. Just call it something else, like "tiered service levels."

Chapter Sixteen

Maintain Visibility through Storytelling

Here's a newsflash: Your organization has attention-deficit disorder. Just because you have constancy of purpose doesn't mean the organization does. New initiatives and projects are like presents at Christmas; they are bright and shiny and interesting in the beginning, but lose their luster quickly after a few months. Because visibility often equates to management support, it is your job as a project leader to keep your project front and center. Otherwise, upper management will get bored and move on to the next "big idea."

Several years ago I ran a project called *Innovator*. It was a bright, shiny initiative that was intended to foster boundary-less collaboration, bold ideation, and new innovation. As with any muscle, collaborative innovation takes thousands of hours of collective practice before it becomes an instinctive organizational competence. My job was to jump start the process.

The rules of engagement were very simple. Submit an idea and people from all over the company, all over the world, would vote and comment on the idea. The voting would allow better ideas to float to the top while the commenting was intended to produce a richer collaboration from multiple eyes. This is nothing new; all of social media, Wikipedia in particular is based on the democratization of collective collaboration.

I put together a huge, splashy campaign. All of the senior executives were featured in different videos urging people to hop onto our site, give ideas, and vote. The teaser was a $10,000 grand prize for the winning idea.

In short order, traffic jumped on our website. Hundreds of employees logged their ideas. Within one month we had 500 unique ideas. About 40% of the company who had access to a computer globally participated in the campaign. There was energy, excitement, and momentum. Then, we selected winners. The winning idea came from a manufacturing engineer who designed a unique coil fed sheet metal shear and laser turret. His idea promised millions of dollars in material savings.

Within one year, the winning idea became reality. Management provided the capital to fund the development and implementation of the idea. There was a ribbon cutting ceremony and the coil fed shear was operationalized, to great success.

Then the recession came and the executive team recoiled to survival mode. They wanted to cancel Innovator but my former boss convinced them to allow me to execute another campaign. However, I had no budget and no support. We executed Innovator with no fanfare, no enthusiasm. People felt that if you were positive and upbeat during a recession that employees would take it the wrong way. Instead, the whole culture emitted a "just get by" mentality. Innovator #2 was a total failure.

Several months later, the CEO held a meeting with his principle leadership team and informed him that he thought their attempts at jump starting innovation deserved an "F" for a grade. Someone asked him what his expectations were. He replied, "I was looking for game-changers, for $100M ideas. I saw none of that." Wow, talk about a mismatch in expectations. He was expecting Steve Jobs sized ideas on part-time and half-hearted efforts.

However, I feel like I failed to properly advocate for Innovator. When I walked around the halls of the company, front line employees kept asking me when the next Innovator campaign was coming out. They really liked the online collaboration. They enjoyed not being bound to their job description. Innovator gave

119

them an outlet to be creative. Since the pace of innovation did not match the executives' impatience for tectonic shifts and revolutionary ideas, they shut down Innovator without allowing the seeds planted in the first year to take full root.

I believe if I could have communicated better what I was seeing on the front lines, the desire from ordinary workers to participate in Innovator, that we could have sustained and grown our collaborative competency.

Carpet bomb the organization with communication

When I received marching orders to lead Pull Replenishment, I vowed not to get sideswiped into the dustbin of indifference again. This time, I would engage in an all-out communications campaign to make Pull Replenishment "feel" big. There would hardly be a week that would go by without the company seeing results from Pull.

The team executed along several fronts. We produced several videos after different kaizen events. They were essentially low-budget rock videos that detailed the challenges we faced, our approach in solving problems, and the results of the kaizens. Shiv and I produced a series of podcasts, educating the company on the benefits of Lean Sigma and Pull Replenishment. We produced several stories for our internal almanac. Every time someone earned his/her green belt, we produced a story. Every time we hit a milestone, we produced a story. We spoke at events. We held conference calls. I briefed small groups. The communication campaign was relentless.

Several people commented, "Wow, you guys are everywhere." Yep. We're not going to let the organization turn us into yesterday's toy. The high point of our communications campaign was the final town hall of the fiscal year. Our CEO asked

Shiv and I to speak and give an update on all the success we had experienced implementing lean and pull. Shiv and I decided the theme of our talks would be "Magic: what vision, leadership, and constancy of purpose can generate in empowered employees."

Tell their story, not yours

As I stood in front of the company, I made sure that I told their story. One communication device I constantly used was to update the number of people who were part of the Pull Replenishment Initiative. It was a collage of faces that I showed during briefings. Every month, the number kept growing. Just like people love hearing the sound of their own name, they love seeing their own face on a slide. Whenever I flashed the slide of faces, people would instantly perk up looking for themselves, as if to reassure themselves that they were important. It was also a subtle way for us to say, "You've been seconded. You are part of the movement."

So at the town hall, Shiv and I kept showing face after face, telling story after story about how everyday, ordinary people produced extraordinary results. My added touch was to play the theme song from "Saving Private Ryan" in the background. The town hall was over an hour long and I was the last speaker. Our internal communications manager shared with me people's reactions:

"David it was amazing. People were getting a little tired. They had been sitting for over an hour listening to speeches. But when you got up there and the music started, everyone sat up and leaned in, all at once. They were mesmerized."

The CEO got up at the very end and joked, "Someday when I grow up, I'll be as creative as David."

For a week people kept coming up to me in the hallways. "That was really great, what you did, giving credit to the team." Their reactions confirmed to me what I've read about public speaking: people don't remember hardly any details of your speech. They only remember how your speech made them feel. I guarantee you, no one remembered any of the technical details of Pull Replenishment, but they remembered the emotion they felt as they listened to stories. And the emotion they *associated* with Pull Replenishment was pride.

Keeping your project front and center is in a nutshell, storytelling. People want to know why what you are doing is relevant to them because in the market place of ideas, only that which is most relevant gets any attention. Storytelling puts a human face to concepts. Honestly, who cares about Lean Sigma, process capability, Pareto diagrams and the like? No one, except Lean practitioners. People care about avoiding pain and maximizing pleasure at their subconscious states. Storytelling taps into that.

Also, storytelling helps people to relate their fears to another's experience. They see and hear stories of courage in the midst of uncertainty and they realize, "O.K., if she can go through this change and still smile, it can't be that bad."

People often think of maintaining visibility as producing better dashboards. Dashboards are effective for certain personality types, those who may have an accounting or engineering orientation. They like graphs and trend lines. That's fine. We customize our communication tools to the intended audience. However, I've found that stories are universally the most powerful tool.

Chapter Seventeen

Believe the best in others

"Dave, I don't want you to get upset, and people won't say this to your face, but many people hope you'll fail." Statements like this always came from well-intentioned friends who didn't want to reveal their sources. I heard this a lot in the beginning but very infrequently once we started demonstrating our success was scalable and replicable. Years ago, I would have heard such words and would have chewed over them like an old piece of leather. But this time around, I learned to shake it off and just believe the best in others and of others.

I determined that no matter if it were true, I would believe that every person I had to deal with was operating out of good will. I chose to believe slights were unintentional and that reasonable people could always work things out.

Constantly focus on the good

What? You say? Aren't you being naïve? Aren't you just overlooking bad behavior? Well, I figured that since I had no control over people's careers and that getting into an arm-wrestling contest would be a losing proposition, I chose to only focus on the good.

My chief modus operandi was the Starbucks card. Even if people had bad behaviors, I believed if I kept recognizing and rewarding good behaviors that sooner or later the good would overwhelm the bad. And that's exactly what happened.

In the beginning of the initiative, people were routinely pushing back their target dates for completing their deliverables. I heard "well, 'this' is dependent on 'that,' and if 'that' doesn't happen, well my 'this' is just going to have to wait until 'that' is done. Over time, people took ownership of the initiative. Since the team generated all of the improvement ideas themselves, each person took responsibility for following through on their deliverables.

In October 2010, we scaled up the number of SKUs we had on Pull Replenishment tenfold. We increased the percent of revenue we were shipping using our build-to-order model from 5% to 50% in one month! By this time, everyone was acting independently, coordinating among themselves all the deliverables they needed to do to make the initiative successful.

I ran into Cheryl one day as she was taking a smoke break outside. We sat and talked about what she was doing. She explained to me in grueling detail the sheer amount of data clean up she was spearheading related to Pull. I did not have this action item as a deliverable on any spreadsheet or project management task list, and yet she was organizing of her own initiative dozens of people putting in hundreds of man hours to ensure that component lead times were accurate within our system.

Many other team members were doing the exact same thing in their own areas, self-directed, unsupervised, yet committed to mission accomplishment. They weren't doing it out of loyalty to me. They were executing to such high standards because they believed in what we were trying to accomplish, felt ownership, and felt empowered to act.

This naturally leads to your question, "What the *heck were you doing?*" I did what the best leaders taught me to do; set your people up for success and get the heck out of their way. Walk the gemba. Observe and encourage. Remove obstacles. Clarify the end state so that actions are aligned. Let your people do the heavy lifting. Let them take all the credit. Believe the best in them and watch them rise to the occasion.

What you believe intensely will manifest itself in your life. Have you ever seen people so intensely hate another person that they start exhibiting similar traits and characteristics? This is called in music and poetry "becoming the one I despise." And yet it is true. I remember seeing privates complain about how a certain sergeant was treating them. They griped and complained, made fun of him behind his back. Sure enough, when they got some stripes on their shoulders, they began to behave exactly the same way. They didn't know any better.

Ill will and Schadenfreude are unfortunately a vicious circle, perpetuated by gossip and water cooler chatter. Even seemingly "helpful" advice can instigate ill thoughts. The only way to break out of this cycle is to choose to believe the best, even knowing that another reality exists. It is when we rise above cynicism, pride, and malice that we empower others to do the same.

Chapter Eighteen

Everything counts in large amounts

O.K., I admit that I am a product of the '80s. I styled my hair like Robert Smith, lead singer of the Cure and listened to new wave music like Depeche Mode. One of their songs is particularly catchy called "Everything Counts in Large Amounts." What I discovered was that breakthrough is really the accumulation of a LOT of small, incremental changes. If you mind the details, the big picture works itself out.

Quick quiz: if you improve something 100% three times in one year, what is the accumulated improvement? And the follow up question: if you improve something 1% per day for one year, what is the accumulated improvement? I will reveal the answer at the end of the chapter.

This chapter is the Ben Franklin-esque list of all the little, practical things you can do as a leader to accumulate huge benefits for your projects:

> **Meeting discipline:** In my experience, a leading indicator that things are not going well is a lack of discipline at meetings. If you don't start and end meetings on time, you are signaling to your team that you don't respect their time. If you don't respect their time, they will not respect meeting deadlines. It's not an infallible rule, but I've seen this play out with remarkable consistency. I always state the purpose of the meeting and the agenda prior to the meeting so that people can arrive mentally prepared. Prior to the meeting, I arrive at the conference room and ensure all miscellaneous

logistics are taken care of: the projector is connected and working, the Breeze link is working, and my presentation is ready to go. If the meeting is a briefing, I always ask people to hold questions till the end. Executives especially are notorious for going off on rabbit trails. I noticed this when I was Director of Strategy. Very quickly we would fall behind by one hour on the agenda and not get to important discussions because someone was reacting to a particular slide. For larger conference calls, I will actually put the call on "silent mode" until Q&A. For working sessions, I monitor "time hacks" so that we don't get off trail. In my mind, meeting discipline is the equivalent of broken windows in a neighborhood. The lack of meeting discipline usually points to a larger problem. Finally, I try as often as possible to give a time dividend by finishing 10 minutes early. It's a subtle reward for starting on time and signals to your team that you care about their time.

Being specific in your communications: Paying attention to what people are doing is absolutely essential. We all have heard the bromides of "Let's please the customer" or "Let's act like a team." When praising or encouraging, you have to get to very specific desirable behaviors. I will point out a certain instance and link what I observed to overall mission accomplishment. "Hey, Jeff, when you quickly called together Person A, B and C to clear up this mess, you really demonstrated the kind of initiative we are looking for. We need to constantly look at how our actions affect those upstream and downstream so that we are all operating on the same sheet of music. Thank you." When I think about the proverb, "Without vision the people perish," I think about clarity. After all what is vision? It is a picture. And the more clear that picture is, the better people will be able to grasp the significance of their actions in light of the vision.

Follow through on your commitments: When I make a commitment to the team, I follow through and communicate my actions. If I let the details slide then I can't expect others to follow through on their end. For example, reigning in expedites has been my particular focus. In terms of bringing Sales leadership, Customer Service, and Operations to the table, I know that as initiative leader that is something I cannot delegate. So, when Customer Service was complaining that we were starting to lose discipline on expedite management, I sprung into action. I worked with our VP and general manager on crafting an executive policy memo to outline how we were going to handle expediting. A group of us re-crafted a quick expedite authorization process to poke-yoke the systemic gaming we were observing. Finally, I personally visited the different Customer Service teams and briefed them on my actions. I knew if they felt that no one was paying attention, they would just mentally quit. Through consistent follow through, we reduced expediting 70%.

Follow up on others' commitments: Sometimes project leadership is simply nagging people to complete their tasks. Many people procrastinate (shocker) and are not skilled at backwards planning, so deadlines will often spring up on them. I try to help by having quick review sessions before a deadline. Now, this can be taken to an extreme. It's like when I was in the Army and before a training deployment we would have our final assembly, let's say at 9:00AM. The company would have an inspection at 7:00AM, the platoon an inspection at 6:00AM, the squad at 5:00AM and the fire teams at 4:00AM. The poor soldiers wouldn't get any sleep. We were in constant hurry up and wait mode. This bred a lot of cynicism towards leadership that people only cared about covering their butts and had no efficient way of doing things. Follow-up should be mostly conversational. One VP of operations asked Bill about his dashboards and Bill replied, "I don't use dashboards. I walk around." When you follow up in person vs. passively waiting to see a dashboard (sanitized of course), people find a new sense of urgency to work on your priorities.

Conduct a daily stand-up: How in the world can anyone stay on top of all the moving pieces? We did this by implementing a 10-15 minute daily stand-up call. This daily discipline brought all the relevant players to the table and surfaced issues before they became a crisis. We coordinated across multiple plants and functions to maintain our 14-day lead times. This best practice was perfected by our "battle captains," Ricardo, Elias, Kim, Melissa, Scott, and Jerry. They faithfully attended the call day in and day out. It took over 6 months of practicing this daily call for us to get our daily dashboards satisfactorily reflecting reality. We updated our Pareto charts in real time so we could analyze root cause issues. I give a lot of credit to our daily stand-up team for maintaining our high level of performance.

Personalize your interactions. Get off your duff and walk. People can handle a 15-minute interruption. They really can. I minimize using email. In this day and age, no one reads email anymore. I make phone calls, a lot. Usually I shoot the breeze for several minutes before eventually moving to the reason for my call or visit. We live in such a dehumanized era of virtualization with Twitter, Facebook, Skype, email and the like. I think people are just craving some real human interaction, or as my wife would call it, "adult conversation." Bill does an exceptional job of this. He constantly wanders the hallways and stops by people's desks. This constant expectation that *Bill might show up* kept everyone on their toes and sharp.

Control email interruptions. Email is the biggest productivity destroyer in the 21st Century in my opinion. People are constantly looking for sensory stimulation and email scratches our sensorial itches. Some people grind through hundreds of emails everyday but you're never quite sure if they are getting anything done. For myself, I try to reduce the number of times I am looking at email to beginning of the day, before lunch, after lunch, and end of day. I try to do real work in between without interruptions. I have never found that there are any emergencies that require an answer within 10 minutes. Most of the time, I can take my time to look at emails, think, and respond within 24 hours. If things are truly important then I will get up and walk over to someone or make a phone call, but email has proven itself truly to be "MUDA" (waste). Consequently, at team meetings and kaizens, we demand that people turn off their cell phones and laptops. If it's important enough for us to meet, then it's important enough to have 100% engagement.

How do you know whether you are sweating out the details or losing the forest for the trees? In my mind, you take your wish list of projects, and whittle them down to the critical few. Once you have defined success for the critical few, no detail is too small. Everything counts in large amounts. You have to demonstrate attention to detail and ensure those critical few priorities complete successfully.

What's the difference between paying attention to details and micromanaging? It's a thin line my friend. One way of knowing is observe your people. If they are demonstrating initiative when you are not looking or not around, then you've successfully empowered people, even as you monitor the details. However, if nothing gets done without you prodding, then your attention to detail is micromanagement.

My friend, everything counts in large amounts. Alright, here's the answer to my quiz: if you improve a process 100% three times in one year, the cumulative improvement is 800%. If you improve that process 1% everyday for one year, the cumulative improvement is 3800%. It's not sexy maintaining constancy of purpose, slowly but methodically improving your corner of the world, but in the long run, the gains are far greater and sustainable.

Chapter Nineteen

Leading – Less and More

I admit the revelations in this book seem obvious and simple. Nothing that we did was intrinsically difficult to do. The difficulty really came in guiding large groups of people through uncharted waters. If it was so simple to actually execute, then why did it take so long? The answer in short, is leadership. In this chapter, I will try to differentiate what leaders do less of and what they do more of that make the critical difference.

It is important to perhaps talk about what many leaders get sucked into that make them marginally effective. The answer is, in short, daily management. I define daily management as forecasting revenue, booking and shipping orders.

Getting sucked into the daily firefighting

When I was a finance leader, I got sucked into this daily management. I spent probably 3 – 4 hours each day reviewing booking trends and forecasting monthly and quarterly revenue. We'd see a spike in orders so the "What's going on?" flurry of emails would begin. We'd see a dip in orders and the "What the heck is going on?" set of phone calls and emails would commence. You see, I was not the only person doing this; this little daily ritual of reviewing booking trends would consume dozens of people's time from Sales to Product Management, Master Scheduling, Operations, Supply chain, Customer Service, and business unit leadership. In short, everyone who eventually touched sales orders got consumed with explaining stochastic, random data.

If you look at the sample data below you will see, that from day to day, the size of our daily bookings was random. So, we'd do all sorts of averages, 5-day, 20-day, anything to see patterns to understand demand variability. Then we'd look at inflection points and ask ourselves, "What do we think the average bookings will be through the end of the month?" I actually got pretty good at this. My financial revenue forecasting accuracy was around 98%.

However, I was merely predicting mid-month what I thought the end of the month would look like. From a capacity-planning standpoint, same month forecasting is pretty worthless. Capacity planning requires a minimum of a 90-day forward-looking view.

Bookings Trends

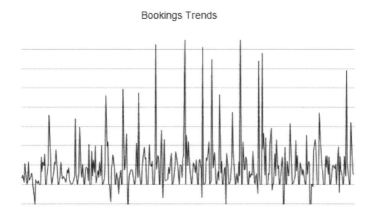

Well, like I said, all of management got sucked up into this game of "What's going on?" Now I'm not saying that forecasting is a worthless activity. Quite the contrary. Capacity planning and forecasting is an essential basic business management skill. However, the sheer number of people who were sucked into the "explaining what's happening" game was overkill, where the interpretation was based mostly on gut and anecdote.

Whenever we tried to start a change initiative, this ritual always took precedence. Noses were buried so deep into daily bookings, shipments, and monthly forecasting, that just to get started required overcoming an incredible mountain of organizational inertia.

To compound this dilemma, organizationally we were spread too thin. We loaded everyone at 120% of personal capacity with key members of projects spending only 10 – 25% on a corporate initiative. Furthermore, we attempted to manage the business globally, resulting in key members of any project team out of country during any given week. Since cross functionally people did not coordinate their calendars, one week person A would be out of office, the next week person B would be out of office and so on. By the time a project team would even meet, six weeks would have elapsed between meetings.

The meetings were fruitless because no one worked on deliverables in between the meetings. So project meetings ended up being long discussions about how much work was left to do. This is what I call the downward spiral of corporate projects. Quarter-end would come around and everyone would drop everything and focus on staring, staring, staring at bookings charts and shipping, shipping, shipping.

Getting out of the daily rut: Strategy Deployment

We had a consultant teach us *hoshin-kanri*, which is Japanese for "strategy deployment." What struck me about the training was the emphasis on where leaders spend their time. In a *hoshin-kanri* managed environment, leaders spend 80% of their time on breakthrough projects and 20% on daily management. In a non-strategy deployed world those percentages were reversed. Guess in what kind of world our company operated?

When managers spend 80% of their time managing bookings and shipments they also start tampering with the process. They believe they can manipulate orders individually and improve delivery. However this is not true. When an ambulance comes blazing down the street, every car pulls off to the side of the road. Tampering is just like ordering an ambulance for a stubbed toe.

So, a strategic leader gets out of this daily management death trap and stays calm in the midst of natural variations without getting sucked into tampering. Bill was such a strategic leader. What's more is he gave time and space to guys like Shiv and me to focus 100% on our initiatives. We were never asked to attend other extraneous meetings nor get sucked into spending our time chasing our tails in "fixing" natural variations seen in bookings and shipments. We focused our time on fundamentally changing our underlying order and fulfillment processes.

Create time, space and tools

Shiv often remarked, "I need time to think. Bill gave us time and space to think." This is so critical. In certain cultures, thinking is viewed as a "lesser" value activity. In certain company cultures, looking busy as a beaver, frantically going from meeting to meeting, working overtime, and meeting on weekends is viewed as synonymous with good management. It takes a very strong leader not to succumb to the appearance of looking busy.

Bill was just the opposite of the overly busy leader. He was like one of those serene jiu-jitsu masters that you can view on YouTube. Certain masters defeat their opponents with minimal effort, minimal movement. The other guy is swinging away wildly, making lots of noises and the master barely pivots and throws the opponent. This idea is captured by Sun-Tzu:

> *Hence to fight and conquer in all your battles is not supreme excellence; supreme excellence consists in breaking the enemy's resistance without fighting.*

That explained Bill and his wonderful Pilates ball sitting, hard-boiled egg eating, shoes off quirkiness. He said, "David, when you get to my age, you can act like you don't care and people will just attribute it to old age." It takes supreme confidence to just be and not care about people's opinions.

That supreme confidence translated into how we ran Pull Replenishment. We calmly viewed the data, analyzed them, and applied Lean Sigma tools as countermeasures. We spent less time spinning our wheels and hence accomplished more. Heck, I got to go home to my wife and four kids for dinner most nights of the week. Less is more.

Let me state emphatically; daily management is important. Someone has to mind the ship. However, moving the business strategically requires leaders to spend less time on daily management and more time on creating new process capabilities. As a leader, you have to carve out time, space, and tools for your people so that they are not forever trapped in the daily sucking noise of crisis management.

Chapter Twenty

Failing is learning

The speed at which we executed Pull Replenishment was blindingly fast. We implemented the initiative in less than one year. This was after four years and millions upon millions of dollars of wasted capital. In our history as a company, we had never completed and end-to-end corporate initiative. When I think about all the lessons I learned, I have to say that failure was my greatest teacher.

When you walk around the halls of the company and bring up the previous initiatives, no one wants to admit they had anything to do with them. Not me. I say very plainly, "I was hired for VECTOR. It was a massive failure. I had many hopes and dreams attached to it, but we failed. I feel like I failed." I'll admit, those first three years were tough. It felt like the Titanic was sinking and no one cared. Almost everyone who was hired for all the different permutations of our company transformation had departed. It wasn't until Bill and Shiv arrived that things started to change.

Bill taught me the importance of authentically caring for the employees. I remember in his very first speech at an all-hands meeting he talked about safety. I will never forget the fact that over his tenure, he has never deviated from safety being his utmost concern. None of this winning matters if people lose life, limb, or eyesight. Bill cared and it didn't take people long to figure that out. So, if Bill cared, then what he said must be good for us. And people worked hard not to let Bill down.

In DDT and VECTOR we did a horrible job communicating that we cared about the employees. We very clearly communicated that we cared about shareholder value. What does the average employee care about the share price of the company?

Most of them didn't have stock. And yet, for the people who did own a lot of stock, getting those who didn't care about shareholder value to care was the only way that shareholder value was going to appreciate. (Isn't that ironic?) However, nothing we said resonated with employees. We utterly failed to communicate the need for change.

We utterly failed to communicate the benefits to the employees. Yes, we can find slides that talk about empowering employees, but no one was buying it. The word on the street was, DDT was a cleverly designed program to justify headcount reduction. And indeed, I sat in on some meetings where the only way management could justify all the effort for DDT was to cut heads. Even if you don't say this, employees are smart and can pick this up.

We utterly failed to communicate the benefits to the customers. As I was in finance, I produced a PowerPoint deck that detailed our transaction costs. It cost us $120 to process and ship an order, $350 to process and ship an expedite and $5000 to create a new part number. I did this through activity based costing. My number circulated around with management. Holy cripes! We create x-thousand new parts every year. If we stopped proliferating new part numbers we would save $10M. Hey! How are we really going to save $10M? <whisper, whisper>, Oh, we would have to cut xxx number of heads. Well everyone feels overworked as it is and no one wants to offer up any heads to chop. Let the product proliferation continue!

People took away from my deck that dealing with customers was a problem. Talking to customers and working with them was very costly. Hey, let's just not have any customers, David, and your problem is solved! It just goes to show that facts plus data does not equal the answer. No matter what the numbers said about the cost of product proliferation, the analysis only incensed people's indignation. "Who the heck are the finance people telling me how to run my business?" "What do they know about customers?" "What do they know about our competition?"

We utterly failed to involve our sales force. We accepted the excuse that they had to hit their quota and so we did not include them. And when Sales finally did learn about the initiative, they felt blindsided and fought against the proposed changes. I saw this pattern happen five or six times with the same result. Our sales organization acted as powerbrokers in the company. They owned the customer relationship and at the end of the day, we did what Sales wanted us to do. Nothing seemed to happen without Sales' approval, but like a dog returns to his vomit, we kept planning things without involving Sales.

We utterly failed to involve people who touched the process we were trying to change. It worked like this: a bunch of executives and senior managers would sit in a conference room for a week and brainstorm ideas. They would pitch their ideas to VP's who would butcher up these ideas and add their own ideas. The amalgamated idea would get passed down and no one would enthusiastically pass it any further. I used to walk around and ask people what they knew about DDT. Nada. It was the largest corporate initiative in the company's history and no frontline employee seemed to have heard of it.

I remember sitting in meetings with the executive team. They were so frustrated. Why doesn't anything cascade down properly through the rank and file? Who are these supposed middle managers that are blocking everything? No one could actually find a blocker, but everyone was sure they existed.

What happened in reality was that no one from top to bottom believed in any of these initiatives. The minute we had difficulty in our core business, let's say dealing with a large quality issue, the executive sponsors themselves proposed dropping the corporate initiatives. It wasn't until Bill and Shiv arrived that the concept of constancy of purpose even existed.

We utterly failed at inspiring anybody. We utterly failed at creating any momentum. We utterly failed at controlling our consultants. We utterly failed at scoping for success. And so on, and so on.

So, when my name got placed next to Pull Replenishment, I did what I felt was logical. I thought long and hard about DDT and VECTOR and did the opposite of what I observed previously. I know this sounds simplistic, but yes, that's what I was thinking. Insanity is repeating the same thing over and over, expecting different results. I decided that at a minimum, I would not be insane. Luckily for me, Bill and Shiv were not insane either.

I used to get so upset thinking about DDT and VECTOR. It galled me to no end to think about all the money we wasted. Then I realized that it was water under the bridge. It would truly be a costly waste if I didn't learn anything from the experience. If I did learn something, it would be an expensive education.

What I took away from DDT and VECTOR was to not get bitter about failure. Without having participated in those failures, I would not have known how to make Pull Replenishment a success. Failing is learning.

Chapter Twenty-One

Authenticity is everything

Find your authentic voice

When I got out of the Army, my first gig was in sales. I supported a megadeal sales guy who had closed several hundred million dollar outsourcing deals in the past. He was trying his darnedest to teach me how to be an elephant hunter, but unfortunately, I had just come out of the Army and I kept saying "yes, sir" and "yes, ma'am" to just about everybody. "Stop doing that," he implored me. "No executive will take your phone call if you talk like that. You have to act like you're their equal. Don't ask for Mr. So-and-So. Say, 'Hi can you connect me to Stan, please?'" So, as a good mentor does, we practiced calling each other. He was in the adjacent office.

Ring-ring. "Hello…" he said gruffly.

"Um, uh, yes, sir, um, can I talk to Mr. Stan Cooper?"

"Damn it, David. I told you to stop that 'yes sir' stuff. I appreciate your service to the country, but you won't close deals if you talk like this."

"Yes, sir."

That was my first lesson in the business world about authenticity. You have to be confident in your own skin and, well, I was no mega-deal elephant hunter. Interestingly, in my next sales job, my territories were overseas and who I was worked. I had to cold call executives in France, Germany, Poland, Czech, literally, all over Europe to set up distribution channels. While I was stationed in Germany, I had learned to speak German and French and used this to my advantage. So, here's my phone call to a managing director in Germany.

"Ja, hallo. Ich möchte mir Herr Schroeder sprechen, bitte."

"Ja, wer ist am Apparat."

"Ich heisse David Choe. Ich rufe von Amerika an."

"Moment bitte."

An American trying to speak German (or French) always worked. They were so blown away that I spoke even a modicum of their language that they always took the call or met me when I was in town. Over time, my confidence increased. It didn't mean the jitters were eliminated. To this day, I hate cold calling, but I found my voice of authenticity.

As I took charge of the Pull Initiative, I had to do things that fit my personality (and still mesh with others') so that I could act confidently. So, when I came up with the idea of recognizing people's positive behaviors with Starbucks cards, I went with it. No one told me to do it. It felt natural. Thank God Bill gave me the latitude to go with my instincts.

In different management books I read how Jack Welch made the handwritten note a mainstay of how he exercised his influence. It felt natural for me to do so, so I did the same thing. I wrote dozens and dozens of hand-written cards thanking people as specifically as I could for their positive contributions to the project. In the card I would include a Starbucks card.

In the Army, unit commanders made custom coins that they gave their soldiers. I took that concept and went to one of the manufacturing managers and asked him to help me develop and manufacture coins internally. His team really bought into this and helped me design coins that we gave out after every kaizen event.

All of these ideas fit my personality. I would sometimes lay in bed thinking of different little knick-knacks and motivators. It sounds dumb, but giving out Starbucks cards and trinkets really motivated me. Looking for the good, finding it, recognizing it, and turning it into a story that I could share gave me great joy. And yet I realize the vast majority of people who read this will never adopt any of these actions specifically.

Indeed, despite the overwhelming, disproportionate success of our Initiative, I know of no other managers who give out Starbucks cards, coins, pins and the like, and that's O.K. What I've learned over the years is that leaders must eventually find their own voice.

I remember a long time ago listening to some Anthony Robbins tapes. Now this guy, as effective as he may be, is way over the top. I tried to act like him, strut around like him. I couldn't do it for even one hour, it felt so silly.

Find your authentic cause

People can smell a phony from a mile away. What makes change agency so difficult is that many people want to know why you want to push change. From their perspective, it looks like you, the change agent, think you are smarter than they are. It looks like they are the ones who have to do all the changing. It can feel like the change agents walk around with a sense of moral and intellectual superiority. It can seem like the change agent is only trying to accelerate his career at their expense.

As I took on the role of leading this change initiative, I had to take a lot of time to reflect deeply on why I was doing what I was doing. Here's what I concluded:

After reviewing the data and the process maps revealing the massive inefficiencies accompanying our order fulfillment process, I concluded that we as leaders were setting up our people for failure. Our business generated less profit than our cost-of-capital and required an enormous amount of overhead. We consumed over 30% of revenue in our operating expenses to deal with the massive complexity we had generated. The reason we were failing our people was that in spite of all the cost built into our model, we still only shipped 65% on time. Customers were frustrated with us. And when financial results were poor and we axed our people, these ordinary workers were only following a hugely inefficient process that management had created. In my mind, this was the height of management failure.

I thought about the livelihoods of all the workers in the company. They all just wanted to make a decent living, raise their kids, and enjoy some of the fruits of their labors. To not change would be to damn them to the whims of the market. Those meditations fueled me to constantly push through all the obstacles we faced, because failing meant people would lose their jobs.

As we completed our first year implementing Pull Replenishment, our financial indicators were the best they had been in over a decade. In a down economy, with revenue lower than in the previous year, our operating profit was up dramatically. We finished the year with everyone receiving his or her largest bonus in a decade.

Finishing the year, I was grateful I to just be a part of all the great accomplishments our people had produced. We changed the culture, we generated outstanding results, and we enjoyed each other's company. How many people can say that?

I dubbed my authentic cause "creating meaningful work." To destroy the circle of death in our order management process enabled our people to do meaningful work. That meant that they could put in a very tough, but manageable 40-hour week, go home, and know they moved the ball forward under the new processes we created. In the old process, people could've worked 100-hours and would have accomplished far less. The old process was nothing more than a non-stop fire drill that ground our people into the proverbial dust.

The highest compliment anyone gave me came from Ricardo. He said, "People know you care." Coming from him, that was high praise and a great reward in itself.

Chapter Twenty-Two

Build a Plurality of Leaders

Usually acknowledgements are given in the beginning, but this time, I included it as a chapter. I use the term "plurality of leaders" versus simply "team" because these leaders had to carry the Pull banner in their respective worlds without prompting, without prodding, and transform their corner of the company.

"Give me a lever long enough and a fulcrum on which to place it, and I shall move the world." So said Archimedes. In the business world leverage usually refers to using debt as a means of financing projects. In the world of leaders, leverage means maximizing the talents of those willing and available. Without leverage a leader is not a leader but simply a manager of resources.

I was fortunate this time around to be surrounded by leaders, who in their own way were smarter and more talented than I. I've already talked at length about Bill, Shiv, and Randy, but what about the others? Here's where I shine a spotlight on some of them:

Ricardo Rodriguez was our director of materials in Juarez. When I started the initiative he was relatively new to the company. Sophisticated and cosmopolitan, he did not fit the typical ADC mold. He wore Gucci and carried Tumi bags, drank expensive whiskey (not at work, obviously) and read more books than I ever contemplated reading. If you ever saw the movie "Pulp Fiction," he was Mr. Wolf. He kicked butt and got things done.

Fab Moroso was a Master Black and principal kaizen facilitator. He led almost two kaizen events per month. As a former Lean consultant, he was used to the frenetic pace of leading kaizen events week in and week out. He exuded knowledge and mastery of the Toyota Way with an impatient energy. I always told people, "In case of war, break glass and Fab will come out swinging." Fab forced people to change and did not accept "no" for an answer. I was constantly amazed at how far he pushed the envelope in getting people out of their comfort zone, but it worked.

Scott Blaine was our supply chain leader. He coordinated and organized the commodity managers to negotiate with hundreds of suppliers to reduce lead times, sign up for consignment or VMI, and ensured that suppliers maintained their commitments. Scott constantly thought of new options, new suppliers, alternative materials and constantly war-gamed in his mind, "What if this goes wrong?"

I can't talk about Kim Haller without Melissa Weigand. They were in charge of master scheduling. I call them the Wonder Twins. Kim finished Melissa's sentences and vice-versa. Whenever I finished talking with Melissa I would say, "Just use your telepathy…O.K.? Alright, now I know Kim just got the message." They epitomized the biblical allusion of oxen being yoked together, meaning two people in sync can pull more than double the load of each individual. Whenever I had Six Sigma Black Belt training to attend to or if I had to travel, I handed the initiative cockpit over to Kim and Melissa.

Cheryl Tiegs was one of our material planners who had to retrain the entire material planning group to shift from a SAP forecast driven methodology to using SAP in support of Pull. That sounds like a mouthful, but it just means people had to change how they did their work. Although they weren't comfortable changing, Cheryl taught as one who was changing with them, at their pace. Ultimately, people followed Cheryl's lead.

Mary Wells was one of our customer service managers. She had to retrain the entire Customer Service department with the "no expedite policy." Because Customer Service acted as a frontline interface between Sales and the customer, they always received the most flak. Mary had to navigate this organization to face their fears and move forward through the change.

Tyler Scott was our resident functional support expert. That means he translated business requirements into SAP-speak and helped us rewrite the business logic of our order management systems. Tyler had to balance the customer experience with reducing internal complexity and performed the work of several IT folk.

I call Elias Cuellar, Rico Suavé. He was a whiz at creating dashboards and reporting tools. Whenever he came up to Minnesota we took him to a local restaurant called Redstone to watch him hunt cougars with his Latin dancing. Elias was a smooth operator.

Another dynamic duo was Joy McKnight and Ben Paasch. Joy was our master of analytics, reporting, capacity planning, forecasting etc. She dreamed up new tools to make everyone's lives easier. Then she turned to Ben. Ben looks more like someone who should be developing online games than someone working in a stodgy telecom company. But, to our benefit, Ben is a master at creating Access databases and accompanying custom tools. Joy would give Ben her set of requirements, Ben would pop on his earphones, listen to some tunes, and crank out whatever Joy asked for.

Ali Habib was one of our Black Belts. He piloted new concepts with one of the product lines and seamlessly tied material flow using bar code scanners. Unless you're a Lean expert it's all heady stuff. Suffice it to say that Ali took us to a whole new level.

Jerry Groen did more before 9 A.M. than most people did all day. He was our distribution warehouse director. I did not understand how talented he was until I compared his performance with other warehouses. Our team took for granted that we gave him just one day to receive goods from our factories and turn those around into customer deliveries. I discovered later on that most distribution centers required three to five days to do the same task.

Bonnie Fromm helped create an internal material flow process to ensure that internally produced parts were built, labeled, and shipped out the door faster. She created a simple process of stamping internal paperwork for Pull, highlighting the jobs using green paper and tying all internal logistics personnel to this process. In a world where minutes count, she shaved off hours of lead time with her simple process.

Mario Dena was the VP of manufacturing at our Juarez facility. You have no idea how difficult it is for a plant manager to allow a team of outsiders to come in and "suggest" improvements. It takes a great man of incredible self-confidence and humility to do so. Thankfully, Mario is one such person. He supported Pull with resources and most of all, his personal stamp of approval. We couldn't have executed Pull without Mario's endorsement. Gracias, señor.

I could go on and on about other heroes who quietly did their work without fanfare. They, along with dozens and dozens of others, started a movement that improved the customer experience, improved profits, and increased employee engagement. Ultimately, my job was to be their cheerleader and to tell their story. I know I haven't done them justice. They deserve all the credit for the success of the initiative.

Epilogue: Where is the Initiative Now?

From strength to strength

All good things eventually come to an end, but for us, the journey is still going strong. Different team members have moved in and out of active participation, but with each passing day, our movement is becoming a part of the culture. No one snickers about Pull going away or wonders aloud when it will fail. The colleagues who touch the process from quoting, order entry, scheduling, materials management, capacity management, operations, warehousing and shipping all continue to demonstrate ownership. What a happy thought! And we continue to gain strength in other areas.

One area we are actively tackling is the distribution channel. Channel partners account for a significant percentage of revenue and shipments but we have not maximized the benefits of using the channel. Instead, we get caught up in a yearly "cycle of doom." Like the circle of death, the cycle of doom causes our employees to go into non-stop firefighting mode but with minimal incremental results to show for all their efforts. The cycle of doom, however, is more painful, because our entire supply-chain is affected by it.

How does it work? Essentially, when order volume is slow in the distribution channel, our partners work to burn off inventory. We see now purchase orders for several months on a particular SKU. We begin laying off workers, cancelling purchase requests with our suppliers. Our suppliers mothball capacity and slow down. Then, around February or March every year, customer orders start picking up. The channel partner looks at the inventory on hand and compares it to the current run-rate and panics. Our partner orders many multiples of the current run-rate as safety stock. This creates a demand spike, an order of such magnitude that neither we nor or suppliers have sufficient capacity or materials to fulfill the order on time. The entire supply chain struggles to fill the order for months until end-customer demand drops.

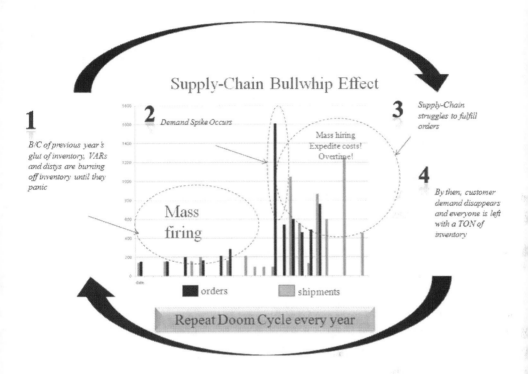

Just as we are fulfilling the orders, the channel realizes that they will have 10x the inventory needed. Distributors start canceling orders and pushing out orders through the end of the year. At the beginning of the year they start out with excess inventory and begin burning off their inventory until February. Repeat cycle of doom.

This phenomenon is so well known and documented. It is often referred to as "The Beer Game," based on a simulation MIT developed. Though the effects of demand spikes are well known, those living in the middle of it, cognizant though they may be, continue to repeat the cycle of doom with compelling predictability.

The way out of the cycle of doom is demand replenishment, which is replenishing inventory in the channel based on usage, not forecast. This sounds very simple and obvious. Indeed Toyota pioneered this concept probably 50 years ago. Walmart and Dell perfected it; the telecom industry sees this as "novel."

Anyway, we have modeled with real data that we can reduce inventory by 50%, reduce hiring/firing costs by 33%, and reduce expediting costs by another 50% by implementing demand replenishment in the channel. Our partners are signing up enthusiastically and I have a full schedule of work for the next decade.

Well, if our channel partners demand spike us, guess what we do to our suppliers? We've initiated pull replenishment with our suppliers and they are already seeing the benefits. With several hundred key suppliers, there's a ton of work left to do.

We're having a LOT of fun keeping the movement going. I'd be happy to hear about and share experiences with you. Drop me a line at david_s_choe2002@yahoo.com. I have faith that with the right team, the right set of tools, and constancy of purpose, you too can start a movement in your company.

9992891R0009

Made in the USA
Charleston, SC
29 October 2011